Fixing Special Education

12 Steps to Transform a Broken System

Miriam Kurtzig Freedman, M.A., J.D.

www.schoollawpro.com
www.parkplacepubs.com

School Law Pro and Park Place Publications

This *little flipbook* is part of the *little flipbooks of laws* series
by attorney Miriam Kurtzig Freedman, published by School Law Pro.

The other titles in this series are

Grades, Report Cards, etc. . . . and the Law (2005, 2008)

IEP and Section 504 Team Meetings . . . and the Law (2008)

Student Testing and the Law (2001, 2004, 2005, published by LRP Publications;
to be reissued in 2009 by School Law Pro)

Contents

Foreword

Miriam Freedman's *little flipbook* is bold and concise, offering big ideas in a commonsense format. Ms. Freedman shares my vision that our country will be much better off with less litigation and fear of litigation in our daily lives. As citizens, we should be able work through challenges together, rather than running to courts to impose solutions on everyone else. Special education is the classic example of good intentions gone awry, as Ms. Freedman argues forcefully.

This book is a must-read for anyone interested in improving special education and restoring balance to school decision making.

Fixing Special Education invites discussion and action. I am happy that Ms. Freedman has shared her wide experience in this compelling little book. I hope that it starts an important national conversation.

Philip K. Howard
Chair of Common Good and author of
The Death of Common Sense

Introduction

M y friend Miriam Freedman is an astute, courageous, and compassionate person. On top of that, she is a fine lawyer. This book represents the thoughtful distillation of her many years of experience with and observation of our special education system.

There are many who are fearful of saying anything negative or controversial about serving students with disabilities. Others have grown so resentful over the way the process has mushroomed out of control that they have lost sight of the law's noble intent and many successes. Miriam maintains a healthy balance, calling for us to celebrate the success of special education services while taking a long, hard look at the problems.

Moreover, she offers solutions. This is not a book of complaints and grievances. It is a book that offers concrete, practical solutions to real challenges.

Some will bemoan the fact that a book about educational services is written by a lawyer, not an educator. But the lawyer takeover of our special education system is the heart of the matter. No one is better situated to diagnose the problem and prescribe the cure than someone who has seen it from the inside.

At Park Place Publications we are hoping that Miriam's book about special education will spark a long-overdue conversation. We are proud to bring it to print.

Jim Walsh
Founder, Park Place Publications

Acronyms and Terms

ADA/ADAA	Americans with Disabilities Act/Amendments (2009)	NCLB	No Child Left Behind Act of 2002
ADD/ADHD	Attention deficit disorder, without or with hyperactivity	OHI	Other health impairment; often ADD or ADHD
child/student	Terms used interchangeably	RtI	Response to intervention—general-education focus on diagnostic teaching, data collection, and outcome analysis of student learning
ED	Emotional disturbance		
ELL	English-language learner		
FAPE	Free appropriate public education		
IDEA	Individuals with Disabilities Education Improvement Act of 2006 (was preceded by the Education for All Handicapped Children Act, known as EAHCA or EHA)	Section 504	Section 504 of the Rehabilitation Act of 1973, an antidiscrimination law. "504 plans" provide accommodations and services.
		SES	Socioeconomic status
IEE	Independent educational evaluation	S/L	Speech/language impairment or delay
IEP	Individualized education program	SWD	Students with disabilities served under the IDEA or Section 504
LD	Learning disability; also called specific learning disability (SLD)	US ED	U.S. Department of Education
LRE	Least restrictive environment		

Fixing Special Education

Executive Summary

On the first day of school on a bright September morning in the late 1950s, my friend's mother took her little sister, Eleanor, to school in New York City. Eleanor was six years old. At the schoolhouse door, the principal waved them away, saying, "We don't educate children like that." Eleanor had Down syndrome. She returned home and never went to school.

Stories like Eleanor's led to court decisions and ultimately, in 1975, to our nation's first special education law, now known as the IDEA—the Individuals with Disabilities Education Act. A product of the 20th-century civil rights era, it ended the exclusion of students with disabilities (SWD) from schools and mandated that they receive a free appropriate public education (FAPE). That was then.

Now some six million students are served under the IDEA, with its entitlements for SWD and their parents. Its history is a dramatic story of success worthy of celebration.

Yet let us acknowledge that, beyond its success, this powerful law spawned a system that is too often focused on legal procedures rather than educational outcomes. It has become dysfunctional, producing a huge bureaucracy and warring stakeholders. Reportedly, it is the *fourth most litigated federal statute.* Clearly, the system is broken.

This *little flipbook* proposes 12 steps for necessary systemic reform, suited for our 21st-century reality. These steps will be easy, hard, radical—and some, perhaps, not politically correct. In the spirit of innovative change, let us consider them all and not fear touching special education. We need to focus attention on the prize— improved teaching and learning for *all students.* Let us have open and honest discussion and confront challenges with boldness, smarts, and creativity that will lead, ultimately, to success. The time is right— especially as more than $12 billion in federal stimulus funds are added to a broken system.

Outline of the 12 Reform Steps

We need CLIMATE CHANGE.
1. End the litigation of a student's special education services (FAPE).
2. Eliminate the fear of litigation that grips our schools.
3. Reduce the bureaucratic morass. Paperwork is not education; documents don't teach.

CHANGE THE PATH we are on.
4. Educate *all* students, without labels. End reliance on the medical model as the gatekeeper for services.
5. Change the role of parents in the law from "law enforcers" back to "parents."
6. Treat inclusion as a means, not the end, of a good education.
7. Focus on the *whole* child—strengths as well as weaknesses.
8. Remind students, parents, and teachers that education is an *active* process.
9. End the overuse of accommodations. Stop lying to students, parents, and regulators.

REBALANCE SCHOOLS for all students.
10. Curb excesses in the law. Educate *all* students, starting from where they currently function.
11. Follow the money for special education and educating SWD—a most challenging endeavor.
12. Create an action plan.

The VISION
Free schools from the bureaucratic stranglehold and fear of litigation so that we can get back to focusing on teaching and learning.

Now, Let's Get Started

Special education needs a fix! This *little flipbook* sets out key issues and a set of 12 proposals to fix special education. We will look at where we are now and how to get back to common sense and educate *all* children. Let us consider solutions—even if they are outside the box (which is a bit wobbly anyway).

President Barack Obama's inaugural speech set out the challenge:

The question we ask today is not whether our government is too big or too small, but whether it works. . . .
Where the answer is yes, we intend to move forward. Where the answer is no, programs will end.

Special education is a mix of the two—parts that work well, and parts that do not.

First, the very good news—
the parts that work well.

We all won! Schools, educators, parents, citizens, officials, communities, students—all of us. From a dark period of excluding many students with disabilities, we have moved to educating *all* students in our nation's schools.

Since 1975 the special education law, first the EHA and now the IDEA, opened the door to fairness and access to schooling for millions of children with disabilities.[1]

Even before 1975, courts and some state legislatures had moved to end exclusions. In the early 1970s, in the *PARC* and *Mills* cases, two district courts mandated the end of exclusions for SWD.[2] They ordered schools and states to implement procedures such as referrals, assessments, recognition of parental rights, individualized education plans, and even due process hearings. In short, they focused on *procedural requirements* for SWD and—for the first time in any law or court decision—*put parents in charge of enforcement.*

And that is how, some 40 years ago, school programs designed in courtrooms by lawyers and judges became the law of the land. The law created entitlements for SWD and their parents that continue to this day. A very powerful law, indeed.

We now educate some six million children under this law. Nearly 14% of all students receive special education services.[3] Originally intended for children with more significant disabilities, special education now includes many other disability groups. It affects all schools and communities in the United States.

It was noble to end exclusions and discrimination. The law changed our vision. We now have an inclusive approach for all students. Even our language changed. The days of using the terms "educable" and "noneducable" are but a very distant memory. The current mantras are "All means all" and "All children can learn." These are huge leaps that our nation undertook. Today many SWD succeed in school. A growing number graduate from high school, go to college, and lead productive lives.

Instead of children being excluded and isolated at home or in separate institutions with little or no chance of becoming independent, taxpaying citizens, many SWD now do exactly that. The civil rights era changed how we include and educate SWD forever. Let's toast our success!

Since 1975, the IDEA has morphed and expanded to include 14 categories of SWD. Some deem this expansion *mission creep*.[4] Others may call it a more inclusive system.

- Autism
- Deaf/blindness
- Deafness
- Developmental delay
- Emotional disturbance (ED)
- Hearing impairment
- Mental retardation
- Multiple disabilities
- Orthopedic impairment
- Other health impairment (OHI), including ADD and ADHD
- Specific learning disability (SLD), sometimes called learning disabled (LD)
- Speech or language (S/L) impairment
- Traumatic brain injury (TBI)
- Visual impairment, including blindness

Erin Dillon of the think tank Education Sector concludes that four categories—SLD, S/L impairment, OHI, and ED—account for more than 70% of all SWD.[5] Fewer than 30% of SWD are designated as having the more severe disabilities, such as mental retardation, deafness, blindness, deaf/blindness, and multiple disabilities—the population of students for whom the law was originally designed.

Wade F. Horn and Douglas Tynan cite even starker numbers: *"Although the federal program was initially intended to address the educational needs of the severely disabled, today approximately 90 percent of special education students have lesser disabilities, such as a specific learning disability, speech and language delays, mild mental retardation, or an emotional disorder."*[6]

The growth in students identified with SLDs has been remarkable—300% since 1976. Today approximately 50% of all SWD are labeled as having "SLD." And estimates are that about 80% of students with SLD are so labeled because they did not learn to read.[7]

Yet we often don't really know which came first: Did the child receive the diagnosis because she was not taught? Or did she have a disability that impeded learning?

This *little flipbook* focuses on the group that includes most SWD—that is, students with SLD, S/L impairment, OHI, and ED.

It leaves discussion of the system for more severely disabled students for another day.

Briefly, the law provides the following rights for SWD and their parents or guardians:

Referral and evaluation. Children who may need special education are referred for an evaluation. Schools are obligated to screen students to "find" SWD.

IEP team. Thereafter the IEP team—made up of educators, administrators, parents, and others—considers whether the student is eligible for special education.

IEP. If the student is eligible, he or she is entitled to an individualized education plan (IEP) that provides a FAPE.

IEE. Parents may be entitled to an independent educational evaluation of their child at school expense if they dispute the school's evaluation.

Individualized services. An IEP is an entitlement. Thus, if the IEP team determines that a student needs specific services or placement, those services must be provided, regardless of availability, costs, school budgets, and so forth.

FAPE. The IDEA guarantees to every eligible student with a disability between the ages of 5 and 21 a free appropriate public education (FAPE). Most states adopted wider age ranges, often starting services at age 3 and ending at 22. One state ends special education at age 26.

Educational benefit. To assure a FAPE, each student receives an IEP that is designed to provide educational benefit through specialized instruction to meet the child's unique needs in the least restrictive environment (LRE).

Parental rights. The law provides parents with rights to request all the procedures set forth above. Parents can enforce these rights at hearings and in the courts.

In terms of costs, as the only *entitlement* program, special education can trump other school services and skew budgets. Special education services are provided and paid "off the top," leaving the remaining funds, time, and efforts for all other students. The rates of growth in the cost and the number of SWD have outgrown the rates for regular education. Where can it possibly end?

Our law and practice today continue to reflect those early court rulings and civil rights–era law. SWD receive IEPs in more than 13,000 school districts in 50 states, Washington, D.C., and the territories, each designed on a case-by-case basis. The process is slow and expensive. Sadly, research is lacking to support this procedures-laden approach as the best way to educate SWD.[8]

To continue on this path into the 21st century is problematic. Why? Because the 1970s decisions and laws solved a specific challenge—the exclusion of many SWD from our nation's schools. Today *no* SWD are excluded. All are served in educational programs.[9] Yet our laws and practice continue to become ever more complex and out of sync with the reality of the times. Such public policy may well be termed mission creep—*keeping on keeping on*, driven by inertia, fear, or lack of creativity and will, while losing sight of the goal: improved teaching and learning for all.

Now, for the challenge.

So, what's bad about success? Why not leave it alone? If it ain't broken, why fix it? Well, the reality is that the special education system *is* broken and needs a fixin'.[10] We are burdened by our success: as special education expanded, so did the unintended consequences. We are now dealing with the "excesses of the civil rights movements" of the 1960s.[11]

> It's time for a *new* approach, the "next generation."
> Just as technology advances with new versions, perhaps
> we can move to **Special Education 2.0—**
> **the transformed 21st-century system.**

A bit of history. To understand the need for change, let's step back in time. For those of us who love history, rereading President Gerald R. Ford's 1975 signing statement in which he predicted many of our current challenges is a humbling experience.

Check it out on the next two pages.

President Gerald R. Ford's Statement on Signing the Education for All Handicapped Children Act of 1975 (December 2, 1975)

I have approved S. 6, the Education for All Handicapped Children Act of 1975.

Unfortunately, this bill promises more than the Federal Government can deliver, and its good intentions could be thwarted by the many unwise provisions it contains. Everyone can agree with the objective stated in the title of this bill—educating all handicapped children in our Nation. The key question is whether the bill will really accomplish that objective.

Even the strongest supporters of this measure know as well as I that they are falsely raising the expectations of the groups affected by claiming authorization levels which are excessive and unrealistic.

Despite my strong support for full educational opportunities for our handicapped children, the funding levels proposed in this bill will simply not be possible if Federal expenditures are to be brought under control and a balanced budget achieved over the next few years.

There are other features in the bill which I believe to be objectionable and which should be changed. It contains a vast array of detailed, complex, and costly administrative requirements which would unnecessarily assert Federal control over traditional State and local government functions. It establishes complex requirements under which tax dollars would be used to support administrative paperwork and not educational programs. Unfortunately, these requirements will remain in effect even though the Congress appropriates far less than the amounts contemplated in S. 6.

Fortunately, since the provisions of this bill will not become fully effective until fiscal year 1978, there is time to revise the legislation and come up with a program that is effective and realistic. I will work with the Congress to use this time to design a program which will recognize the proper Federal role in helping States and localities fulfill their responsibilities in educating handicapped children. The Administration will send amendments to the Congress that will accomplish this purpose.[12]

President Ford warned against

- Promising more than the law can deliver
- "A vast array of detailed, complex, and costly administrative requirements"
- Use of tax dollars "to support administrative paperwork and not educational programs"[13]

Rather amazing, isn't it? Prescient. And sad.

Ford's optimism that within three years Congress would develop an "effective and realistic" program before implementing the law was unfulfilled. By 1978 he was out of office. Congress did not streamline this law, and here we are. In fact, the law has become ever more complex and its bureaucratic requirements more burdensome.

Anthony Lewis, a Pulitzer Prize–winning *New York Times* reporter and columnist, tells the story of Justice Hugo L. Black, who thought that all government departments and agencies should be abolished every 5 or 10 years: *"Black was a senator from Alabama for ten years and a Supreme Court justice for thirty-four, and he knew just about everything there was to know about how government works. His startling idea—and I think he was serious— was his solution for dealing with the encrustations of bureaucracy."* [14]

"Encrustations of bureaucracy." An appropriate phrase, indeed.

Where Are We Now?

Well, we know a lot about where we are . . .

We know that the law tasks parents with the job of enforcing it, an approach that can be viewed as a basic and pervasive "structural design flaw."[15]

- It forces parents to fight against schools and assumes that all parents can do so, although many cannot.
- It is inequitable—between savvy parents and others, and between parents of SWD and other parents.
- It creates battlegrounds in our schools instead of fostering the cooperation that should exist between school and home.

This design flaw causes many of the law's unintended consequences. Consider this testimonial ad for a training conference for SWD advocates and parents from www.wrightslaw.com.

> *"What a marvelous conference! I often leave sped [special education] presentations angry and/or guilty because of all the things that were done or not done. This time I left encouraged, inspired, and armed!"*

Armed! Against whom? Is this really what we want or need in our schools?

We know that SWD and their parents are the *only* persons with entitlements in our schools. Other students—including those who are "at risk," English-language learners (ELLs), gifted, talented, bored, advanced, slow, dreamers, socially maladjusted, and so on—receive targeted services only when school budgets allow. And their parents? While they can opine about their children's programs, they have no legal right to assert claims or demand services.

We know that the law often elevates process over outcomes, and bureaucratic rules over achievement and results. Although IEPs are supposed to guide students' educational services, a *"strikingly high number of parents, teachers and administrators . . . have described how IEPs are focused on legal protections and compliance with regulatory processes."*[16] Alas, not teaching and learning.

Back in 2002, the **President's Commission on Excellence in Special Education** found more than 814 IDEA procedural monitoring requirements for compliance by state and local programs and concluded that *"educators spend more time on process compliance than on improving educational performance of children with disabilities."*[17] That's no surprise. Yet, in the ensuing years, the situation has not improved. Congress and the U.S. Department of Education (US ED) have added more complexity, while touting "paper reduction."

Add to that the state and local requirements. These laws overregulate and make education far too complex. The definition of "red tape" is "official routine or procedure marked by excessive complexity which results in delay or inaction."[18] Need we say more?

Can education thrive in such a climate? No, it can't.
We need climate change!

And now for the wider picture . . .

We know that when we look at special education through the wider lens of education in general, it looks rather different. While special education expanded, the wider education world did not stand still. Indeed, it learned much from special education. Consider the No Child Left Behind Act (NCLB), which targets education services for struggling students. Its "response to intervention" (RtI) approach in general classrooms adopted many approaches used by special educators: the focus on individual students, data collection, and research-based approaches. The innovation here is to intervene in early grades in general education classrooms so children can learn to read and do math and so they may not need special education at all! That is, the goal is to end the "wait to fail" model that has plagued special education.[19]

Consider whether RtI would exist today without special education's example and approach. It's rather doubtful. Such cross-fertilization benefits students everywhere.[20]

Mutual and powerful cross-fertilization between these laws continues. The NCLB's focus on academic standards and outcomes targets *all* students, including SWD. Its requirement for research-based instruction and accountability for *all* children has changed IEPs throughout the land. Thus, today's IEPs include research-based instruction, SWD participate in state and district testing programs, and schools are accountable for the achievement of SWD. This is all to the good.

Madeleine Will, a special education pioneer and advocate famously testified, *"[The NCLB is] more than an accountability statute; it is the institutional embodiment of the high expectations that students with disabilities need to succeed."* [21] Again, convergence between these laws makes good sense and, presumably, leads to better outcomes for students with disabilities.

Another bit of history. Back in the 1970s, the law created two education systems—regular and special. Special education was going to use IEPs to "fix," "cure," and "educate" SWD. Often it succeeded and students benefited. But, over the years, Congress concluded that special education was based on low expectations and did not hold students with disabilities to high standards. Thus, in 1997, Congress revolutionized how we do special education. It mandated that students with disabilities be educated in the *general curriculum* and meet state and local standards. Since then, the law mandates that regular educators attend IEP team meetings.

Yet today, more than 10 years later, instead of working to create a single, unified education system for all students, we still run two systems. Their myriad overlapping and confusing requirements and categories of programs creates bedlam for schools. Stanford professor Michael W. Kirst has described the situation in education in general as "hardening of the categoricals." [22]

Maintaining two systems when we need only one good one is sad and costly. We know that **the better general education is at providing excellent teaching and learning for *all* students, the less special education is needed.** We need to focus on that reality instead and to build one great public education system for all students. That's just the way it is. [23]

Besides lacking the benefits of a unified and focused education system, these two systems create bureaucracies with layers of rules and procedures.

Consider that, reportedly, 43% of education personnel in the United States are teachers. In other countries, 70% to 80% are teachers.[24]

It makes no sense. One set of rules—for general education/NCLB—is driven by state and local standards and accountability standards. The other—for special education under the IDEA—is driven by the individualized FAPE. Two different and opposite approaches for the same students with disabilities. No wonder teachers, parents, and the rest of us are mightily confused.

It's not always a happy marriage between general and special education. Often the laws collide. And amazingly, in this day of research-based instruction as mandated by *both* the NCLB and the IDEA), *no* **research** demonstrates that this dual (and dueling) approach is an effective way to educate our students.

Instead of this broken system being fixed, another strange thing happened. Even as the NCLB and general educators learned from and adapted special education's approaches, they also moved beyond special education. They now focus on data-driven results and outcomes, while special education is still largely about regulations full of procedural requirements. Special education continues to be mired in 20th-century, procedures-laden thinking, which is awkward in the results-oriented 21st-century world. But that's the way it is.

In addition, all states have their own laws for educating all students—including SWD. Again, more **overlap, redundancy, confusion.**

While there may be areas of constructive overlap between these laws and approaches, much confusion and contradiction remains.

We know (or think we know) that special education is expensive. It costs about two to four times as much to educate SWD as it does other students.[25] This amounts to huge sums of money—between 20% and 40% of school budgets nationwide.[26]

We know that accurate expenditure figures are elusive. For one thing, it is not always clear which costs are counted: the costs of special education (lower) or of educating SWD (higher). The latter are higher, because most SWD receive regular *and* special education services. Cost measures should (but may not) reflect that reality. Also, it has become virtually impossible to untangle federal, state, and local costs, under the myriad formulas and mandates that apply.[27]

One researcher concluded: *"Data on special education from all levels of government—local, state, and federal—are fragmented, compartmentalized, and in many cases, inaccessible."*[28]

Whither accountability and transparency? Why do cost data remain so elusive? Perhaps we should look at who wants to know the costs—and who doesn't.

23

We know that much of the new money authorized for education reform ends up funding special education, because of its entitlement status.[29]

We know that the public is largely unaware of or misinformed about these costs. A Phi Delta Kappa/Gallup Poll in 1996 noted, *"Only 7% of [the public] are aware that it costs at least 100% more to educate a special education student than it does to educate an average public school student. Although 17% of Americans do not venture a guess as to the additional costs for special education, fully three-quarters mention a percentage even lower than the estimated 100%—most of them much lower."* Since 1996, the costs of educating SWD are estimated at 100% to 200% higher than the costs for general education students.[30] And the public typically doesn't know that most funds come from local school districts, not federal or state governments.[31]

We know that there are huge inconsistencies from state to state in terms of how many students are identified as needing special education. For example, among 6- to 17-year-olds, the range is between 9% and about 18%.[32] How can this be? What accounts for the variability?

We know that although the law was enacted largely to educate children with severe disabilities, close to 70% (and perhaps more) of the students it now serves have relatively milder disabilities—such as SLD, S/L impairment, ED, ADD, or ADHD. Many folks argue that this growth in serving the more mildly disabled shortchanges the very students for whom the law was intended—the 30% who are more severely disabled.

24

Digging further, we know that some reports indicate that 90% of the students labeled as having an SLD are so labeled simply because they did not learn how to read.[33] Yet, with the IDEA and the NCLB, we now have two competing systems to educate the same students—each trying to teach them to read, do math, and understand science. An unworkable situation.

We know that minority students are overidentified in general and are also overidentified in specific categories, such as mental retardation, ED, and developmental delay.[34] As far back as 1994, the *New York Times* ran a front-page story titled "Special Education Seen as a Trap for Many Minority Students."[35] Apparently such overidentification is ongoing, as highlighted in findings made by Congress in the 2004 IDEA.[36]

We know that special education litigation continues to thrive, in part, because, after some 35 years, we still don't have a definition of a FAPE. What is an "appropriate" education after all? We continue to fight about its meaning on a case-by-case basis. These arguments have created a growth industry for lawyers (including yours truly), "experts," and others. Often referred to as a cottage industry, it may more aptly be called a mansion industry.

25

We know that parents (particularly in affluent communities) use this law to seek public funds for private schools. Professors Thomas A. Mayes and Perry A. Zirkel have observed, *"These lawsuits for reimbursement for private school tuition [are] one of the most controversial aspects of special education law."* They note that school districts are becoming *"increasingly financially strained by . . . the increased frequency of tuition reimbursement [lawsuits]."* [37]

Disputes arise, in part, because the law specifies less than parents may want. While parents may seek what is "best" for their child, the schools are required to provide only what is "appropriate." The Sixth Circuit Court of Appeals famously compared the law's limit to a well-tuned Chevy, not a Cadillac—and not a lemon, of course. [38] Unsurprisingly, disagreements ensue.

In all of this, parents are forced to "advocate" **for** their child **against** the school. They cannot be blamed for doing exactly what the law mandates. Instead, **let us transform the law.**

26

We know that litigation is often a rather ugly process. Consider the Supreme Court's disturbing (incendiary?) language in *Schaffer v. Weast*, a case about the burden of proof in special education litigation. Although parents usually bring the lawsuits and thus have the burden of proof, the Court wrote that they are not powerless, because they have a right to an independent educational evaluation (IEE):

> *IDEA thus ensures parents access to an expert who can evaluate all the materials that the school must make available, and who can give an independent opinion.* ***They are not left to challenge the government without a realistic opportunity to access the necessary evidence, or without an expert with the firepower to match the opposition.***[39] (Emphasis added)

"Firepower" to match the "opposition"? Did the justices forget that we're talking about schools here? Schools are **"the opposition"**? And we thought that schools and parents were **partners** in education. How naive of us. The fact that these two parties have to work together seems lost on the Court.

How sad is that?

27

It's important to remember that these legal battles are unlike many others. When most lawsuits end, the parties never see each again. This "war" between schools and parents damages the relationship and sense of trust between them—the basic trust that forms the foundation of an appropriate education.

We know that without basic trust, achieving a good education is much harder. Yet our system expects educators and parents to testify against each other on Monday, say, and go back to a cooperative relationship on Tuesday. Many teachers cry. Many parents cry. Many teachers quit. This situation impedes efforts to recruit and retain special education teachers—to the point that recruitment is becoming something of a national crisis. The litigation quagmire has dire consequences.

Attorney Christopher Borreca's provocative article entitled "The Adversarial Process: Does It Help or Hurt Our Mission?" tells us:

> *The true answer in restoring the trust between school and parent lies not in creating more enforceable rights but in rethinking the enforceability mechanism itself. As Neal and Kirp recognized early on . . . , "Special education teachers now find themselves as 'defendants' in due process hearings . . . a marked change from their self-perception as lone advocates for the handicapped child."*[40]

Much is lost without basic trust.

We also know that even beyond litigation itself lurk the threat and fear of litigation. This fear permeates our schools, forcing teachers to practice defensive education and spend hours on paperwork to document everything they see, do, and say. Let's be honest. Writing takes time—time away from teaching and learning. Nevertheless, this attorney's advice has been, *"If it's not in writing, it did not happen."*

Philip K. Howard's book *Life without Lawyers* sets out the dilemmas we face when we use litigation to solve everyday challenges. And the nonprofit Common Good has done excellent work regarding these issues.[41]

Some of us know that the law seems to have tipped beyond its goal of opening doors and providing opportunity to SWD. Now it provides some SWD with unfair advantages in several instances. Consider, among other realities, student expulsions during which general education students may be denied educational services but SWD continue to have an entitlement to a FAPE; transition planning that is provided by law for SWD as they prepare to leave high school, but not for other students; and accommodations that include allowing some SWD extended time on the SAT or ACT without informing colleges and schools that testing conditions were altered.

But what we still don't know is whether the current special education system is effective in promoting learning. Do all those procedures and requirements improve or impede learning? In fact, we have not really agreed on what to measure, or for which students. Should it be high school completion? Individual progress? Passing state tests? Being happy? Dropout rates? College completion? Getting a job? And, adding to the quandary, the IDEA and the NCLB have different goals and measures.

30

CommonWealth Magazine's spring 2009 article led with this worrisome banner: *"The cost of special education in Massachusetts is approaching $2 billion a year, but there is little evidence that the state's huge investment is paying off as hoped."*[42]

Some 35 years after the law was enacted, how can this be? The system is broken. Off the rails. Dysfunctional. **Pick your term.**

We also know that we have studied these issues for years. Commission after commission. Study groups galore. Think tank after think tank. All proposing great solutions that often end up abandoned, gathering dust on shelves. Among the studies are these:

- We've had the **President's Commission on Excellence in Special Education**'s *A New Era: Revitalizing Special Education for Children and Their Families.* That was back in 2002, and here we still are, even after the IDEA was reauthorized in 2004.
- We've had ***Rethinking Special Education for a New Century*** by the Fordham Foundation and the Public Policy Institute, a thought-provoking exploration by all sides of the political spectrum. Among its findings: *"Hardly anyone seems pleased with the special education system, yet hardly anyone seems clear about how to fix it."*[43] That was back in 2001, and here we still are.
- We've had Education Sector's "Labeled: The Students behind NCLB's 'Disabilities' Designation" (2007).
- We've had the Public Policy Institute of California's *Students with Disabilities and California's Special Education Program* (2009) and other studies focusing on finances and due process litigation.
- We've had reports by the Massachusetts Association of School Superintendents.
- We've had studies by the Center for Special Education Finance, the Special Education Expenditure Project (SEEP), Brookings Institution, and the American Institute of Research (AIR).[44]
- And many others.

31

A drumbeat of signs has been warning us that the special education system has gone awry. But too many of us chose to ignore the signs and just keep on keeping on. It's reminiscent of the Wall Street debacle that "no one predicted," despite the indicators that were overlooked while the good times rolled.

Yet we continue to study and ponder and study and ponder and study special education and then ponder some more.

Of course, the studies have generated lots of important and interesting questions: Is there enough money? Did Congress promise more, and should it appropriate more? Do parents (or schools) need more (or fewer) rights? How do we keep SWD from dropping out of school?

But we often fail to ask **the *only* question that really matters:**

Does this law of entitlements, procedures, due process, and bureaucracies improve learning opportunities for SWD and for *all* students? Or is it fraught with unintended consequences that harm them all?

33

What to Do?

So, what do we do? We already know enough. It is now time to transform, reinvent, regroup, and be creative and courageous to bring sanity back to our schools. Perhaps we should adopt Google's mantra:

Focus on the user. Everything else will follow.

In our case, the users are *all students*. Focus on them. Everything else that is good for education will follow.

Why did all the studies, research, and commissions not lead to systemic change? Given all that we know, why have no steps for real reform and transformation taken off? Is special education just too hot, controversial, and polarized? No one wants to touch it. Instead, we continue to nip and tuck around the edges, making incremental changes when the law is reauthorized or a court renders a new decision. We just *keep on keeping on*—muddling through with a broken system. Instead, let us do what President Obama urged in another context (the Middle East):

It is time for us to act on what everyone knows to be true.

Indeed, it is.

34

Some thoughts on **why we have become so stuck . . .**

- Perhaps nobody wants to be labeled in some unpopular or politically incorrect way, as being insensitive or uncaring or **anti**-child, **anti**-SWD, **anti**-parents, **anti, anti, anti.**
- Perhaps it is just the fear of change.
- Perhaps it is the fear that, simply by touching special education, we will somehow revert to the pre-1975 exclusion era. This false fear creates a paralyzing false choice.

Let us be crystal clear.

Reforming special education is *not* an invitation to return to pre-1975 days. Education and the world have changed since then. Constitutional protections apply to all students now. We live in an inclusive society. Standards and accountability apply to *all* children. There is no turning back.

What if, instead, we view transformation and reform as a positive, as being **pro** instead of anti: **pro**-child, **pro**-SWD, **pro**–all students; **pro**-parents, **pro**-teachers, and, most importantly, **pro**-learning, **pro**-achievement, and **pro**-success for all students?

35

Indeed, it is long past time for us to gather our courage and have our own "March of Dimes moment" to transform special education *and get with the 21st century.*

Another bit of history. In 1938, President Franklin Delano Roosevelt started the National Foundation for Infantile Paralysis (now known as the March of Dimes), hoping to discover a vaccine to stop the spread of polio. Polio was a dreaded scourge at the time, and President Roosevelt was believed to have had it.

36

Roosevelt's vision caught on. People collected dimes toward the cause. Lots and lots of dimes. Scientists got to work.

In 1955, almost 20 years later, **success!** The Salk and Sabin vaccines were developed.

Thereafter the March of Dimes reinvented itself. It did *not* continue to look for another polio vaccine. It changed its mission and moved on. Now it works on premature birth, birth defects, and infant mortality.

And to this day, our dimes carry the picture of President Roosevelt.

Isn't it time for us in special education to consider changing our mission and moving on? Having succeeded in our 20th-century mission of providing access to schooling for all SWD, with the procedural requirements it entailed, we need to move on to the 21st century and focus on improving educational outcomes for all students. We can do this in three ways:

- Let teachers teach and students learn.
- Get lawsuits and lawyers out of classrooms.
- Let parents be parents, not enforcers of a law that achieved its purpose many years ago.

It is time to bid adieu to the old process-laden, input-based system and focus on America in the new century. We should have done this in the last century. We didn't. Meaningful reform for *all* students—through fairness and excellence—is long overdue.

To paraphrase the philosopher Hillel:
If not now, when? If not we, then who?

38

But How?
The 12 Reform Steps

It's time for a *transformation*. And that transformation can be accomplished in **12 reform steps.** Some of these steps are hard—they involve changing hearts and minds. Some require legislative action. Some are creative and innovative. Some may be easy. Others may be edgy and "out there" and perhaps not politically correct. But let's consider them all.

Remember: These steps focus on the 70% or so of SWD whose disabilities are generally considered to be milder—SLD, ADD/ADHD, language disabilities, emotional disturbance, etc.

Let's divide these reform steps into three categories:

A. **The need for CLIMATE CHANGE**
B. **The need to CHANGE THE PATH we are on**
C. **The need to REBALANCE SCHOOLS for all students**

39

A. We need CLIMATE CHANGE.

Too often, the climate in special education these days is frigid, with too many educators and parents locked in disputes (or threats and fears of disputes) about student placements and FAPE. This climate obscures a painful lack of fundamental trust among all players and results in destructive barriers to teaching and learning. We all know that positive relationships and cooperation among teachers, parents, and students are essential for excellence in education. Yet our current broken system trends in the other direction.

It is beyond irony that this law—lo, these many years ago—envisioned cooperation among all adults. It's time for us to change the climate and get back to that vision.

40

1. End the litigation of a student's special education services (FAPE).

Although due process litigation may have been appropriate in the early days of special education law, it no longer is.[45] It is dysfunctional to continue to litigate educational programming one child at a time. Lawyers, judges, and outside "experts" should not be the ones to choose reading programs or to decide how to teach a child with autism. Education professionals, with due consideration of parents' concerns, should do so. They are far better equipped for that job than are lawyers and judges. It's time to let them at it.

41

Where we are now.

For starters, let's look at some fairness issues.

Is it fair? "Labeled" children "deserve" more services than other students and can sue to enforce determination about and delivery of those services.[46]

Is it fair? Teachers have to spend time to document, document, and document everything they say and do—lest something slip by and bite them in future litigation. Is this fair to teachers? And is it fair to *all* the children they teach?

Is it fair? Litigation and settlement agreements often transfer public dollars from schools to parents, usually to savvy middle- and upper-class parents.[47] It's actually a backdoor voucher program, even in places that don't have one officially.[48] Is this fair or effective education policy?

42

Is it fair? Many cases settle out of court through an agreement between parents and schools to share the cost of private schools or services.[49] The school contributes funds to the parents' chosen program in order to avoid the costs of litigation. Money is transferred from public school funds to the folks who can "pay to play." Some parents can afford to "shake the apple tree" and see what comes down. Other parents can't. SWD whose parents are not effective "advocates" or can't afford to get into the game are left behind.

Is it fair? Parents of SWD can use the state's appeals and court systems to demand services while other parents have no such entitlement. Today, when all children have access to education, why does this inequality continue? As I work in schools around the country, I have asked this question for years and have received no answer.

Some folks respond by throwing up their hands and saying, "Ah, then, let's give all parents due process rights to bring lawsuits and demand services." *Shudder.* More litigation and a more adversarial climate in our schools are exactly what we don't need. We need less of both so we can support more teaching and learning.

Yet IDEA litigation continues. As Perry Zirkel has noted, *"while the trend in education litigation overall has been steadily if not steeply downward since the 1970s, the segment specific to special education has moved dramatically upward during this same extended period."*[50]

Okay. So maybe we can agree that litigation is not fair.

But is it efficient and does it work well? Hmm. Let's see.

The law intended that decisions about special education placements of students be quick and informal. They were not supposed to be formalized, contentious, and long. Alas, they often are.[51] While, by law, SWD usually continue to receive services during the litigation, we can only wonder what the detrimental effect is when the adults in their lives fight over them. Beyond anecdotal data, I am unaware of research on this unintended consequence.

Consider the Supreme Court's *Forest Grove School District v. T. A.* decision in 2009, which awarded reimbursement to parents for their child's private placement.[52] The Court based its decision on several factors, *including the fact that the legal process takes too long*. Oh my.

Here's the timing the justices faced:

2003—The parents sought a due process hearing.
2005—The district court issued its ruling.
2008—The student graduated from high school.
2009—The Supreme Court issued its ruling, six years after the lawsuit started.

The Court said that the ponderous nature of due process review is one of the shortcomings of the law's procedural safeguards. *Agreed.* But then it took a leap to "avoid detriment to the child's education" by billing the school and reimbursing the parents. How exactly does that benefit her education? She had already left school. And what about **fairness** to the schools and taxpayers stuck in this system?

44

Neither schools nor parents created this flawed, out-of-control system. Yet they are both trapped there. Congress created the system, and the courts continue to feed it, adding layers of complexity across the nation. It is time to end this unwieldy and damaging system—not to keep using it as an excuse for further unfairness.

And is it good public policy? More than 30 years after we started down the path of litigating student placements, we have no research or evidence to show that this 1970s legalistic model is the best way to ensure quality education for SWD. Hearings, focused on one child at a time, take an inordinate amount of time and expense, create "battles of the experts" in our schools, paralyze schools and parents for weeks and months (sometimes years), and create winners and losers. They do not promote equity and excellence. They are costly and take precious time and attention away from classroom teaching and learning for *all* students.

Doesn't this situation clamor for change?

45

Where we need to be instead.

- **Define FAPE once and for all.** Answer the question, what is an "appropriate education"? Schools and parents will take it from there.

  The former director of special education in Columbia, Missouri, testified to Congress regarding the 2004 IDEA reauthorization: *"Reform needs to occur when a law is so vaguely written that litigation is required to give it definition. The IDEA is such a statute. Due process is a brutal system. It paralyzes the educational system; it paralyzes individuals."*[53]

  Isn't it obvious that more than 30 years of litigation to try to define a term is long enough?

- **Let educators teach—without fear of litigation at every turn.** In the approximately *180 six-hour school days* per year, we need to encourage teachers to focus on building knowledge and skills, not on preparing documents to build an evidence trail. Decisions about teaching methods and services should be left to schools, not to courts and lawyers. **Pedagogy, not legalism, should drive programs.**

46

Without litigation, a question may arise: **who will protect SWD and their parents?** That's a hard question, perhaps. Let us attempt to answer it. First, in this era, when many laws, including the NCLB and state and local laws, are designed to provide *all* children with appropriate education, is such protection still needed? If so, why? Why do only SWD need an entitlement to educational protection *from* their teachers and schools? Second, assuming that a valid reason for litigation emerges, schools can respond creatively. For example, (a) they can hire an educational *ombudsman* who will help them, with parental input, to determine the appropriate placement. Or (b) they can agree with the parents on a *"second-opinion"* consultant.[54] Or (c) they can have a *public advocate* assist them on an ongoing basis with challenges regarding all students, including SWD. Surely we can create other creative and positive approaches.

We need to ask and explore questions like these. Change is hard. Trust needs to be rebuilt—one step at a time.

Philip K. Howard writes in *Life without Lawyers* that we should abandon the use of litigation through the due process model for social services:

> *The Supreme Court must do its part to remedy this overflow of rights. All the superstitions about due process in schools and public institutions need to be rejected in no uncertain terms. The Court has already moved in this direction by watering down the due process rulings. Now it needs to take the last essential step toward clarity and confirm that daily choices in schools have no constitutional overlay. Schools henceforth will be accountable by decisions of duly elected officials or their nominees, not in lawsuits.[55]*

47

F or special education, Howard's words resonate. This will be a difficult shift, no doubt, as Howard points out:

> *No group wants to give up its rights. Zealots will chain themselves to front doors and scream injustice when we try to restore balance instead of unlimited rights. Perhaps you and I too would feel this way if we shared their predicament. But the overpowering sense of entitlement doesn't make it right. Democracy aspires to balance, not zealotry.[56]*

Of course, if we can't end litigation by going cold turkey, stopgap measures may ease the transition. Beyond the suggestion of an ombudsman, can't parties at least agree to hold off litigation for a reasonable time, to give schools and students breathing room to work together without fear of a lawsuit?

Creative, open-minded problem solvers—we need you!

It is time!

48

2. Eliminate the fear of litigation that grips our schools.

Life without Lawyers opens with these haunting words:

> *"Sometimes I wonder how it came to this," a teacher in Wyoming told me, "where teachers no longer have authority to run the classroom and parents are afraid to go on field trips for fear of being sued." Thomas Jefferson might have the same question. How did the land of freedom become a legal minefield? Americans tiptoe through law all day long, avoiding any acts that might offend someone or erupt into a legal claim. Legal fears constantly divert us from doing what we think is right.*[57]

Tyce Palmaffy writes in a chapter of *Rethinking Special Education for a New Century:*

> *Legal actions (and the threat of legal actions) by parents have led to a backlash, both from special education's critics and from advocates for the disabled. School administrators complain about having their professional decisions challenged by parents and having to worry more about administrative hearings than the actual quality of services being given to students.*[58]

People of good will created this system. They can transform it.

Where we are now.

Is it fair? Often teachers are put on the stand at hearings or in court to testify about education they *will provide* the student. Ask yourself how many doctors or architects, for example, would tolerate that intrusion before they ever performed a surgery or designed a building. It demoralizes educators and destroys the very professionalism we seek to foster.

Is it right? The fear of litigation drives education and expands services for all SWD, according to a study by Thomas Hehir and Sue Gamm. The authors contend that critics of the IDEA focus too much attention on hearing decisions and not enough on all the hearings that don't occur because of settlements: *"The threat of a hearing is an essential element in the relationship between districts and parents because it raises the stakes in disputes over placement."* [59]

50

When special education teachers leave the field, they often cite these reasons: burdensome paperwork and the negative, adversarial climate in our schools. These concerns are tied together, since paperwork is often part of the defensive practices teachers undertake to document their efforts, lest a lawsuit or threat of a lawsuit emerge. Regarding the paperwork burden, see, for example, "Reducing Special Education Paperwork," which states: *"The amount of paperwork that special education teachers are required to complete can contribute to job dissatisfaction and may be a principal cause of teacher attrition."*[60]

At the first annual Special Education Day celebration in 2005, educators responded to an informal survey about their special education concerns. High on the list were these:

- Burdensome procedures, complexity, red tape, adversarial climate, and litigation.
- Loss of trust/respect/dignity between school and home
- Need for another venue for dispute resolution
- Need for regular and special educators to share responsibility and collaborate. The mantra is, "These are all *our* children"
- Need for collaboration among schools, colleges, parent advocacy groups, hospitals, and other evaluators[61]

And consider another benefit if litigation about a FAPE were to end. Among the unintended consequences of our adversarial climate is that educators have let go of their natural inclination to advocate for SWD.[62] Teachers went into the field not to become defendants at trial but to educate and, yes, to advocate for their students. The adversarial climate has eroded that natural, positive inclination. We need to regain it.

Where we need to be instead.

• Let parents be parents instead of being law enforcers.

• Free teachers to teach and students to learn.

• Get lawyers out of the classrooms.

• Encourage teachers to advocate for their students.

• Focus on the achievement of all students.

It is time!

3. Reduce the bureaucratic morass. Paperwork is not education; documents don't teach.

Most folks agree that bureaucracy gets in the way. No evidence suggests that it advances student achievement.

Congress actually tried enacting a paper reduction law, but its effects were minimal. Any law that, back in 2002, had 814 provisions for compliance by public agencies cannot be simplified. *It should be thrown out*, and we should start anew. Kind of like the tax code. The "encrustation of bureaucracy" leaves teaching and learning behind.

Where we are now.

Let's be honest. Even under the best of circumstances, there is *no* way that states and schools can comply with all these requirements. Indeed, the 2000 report of the National Council on Disability, *Back to School on Civil Rights*, found noncompliance in every state.[63]

Educators spend precious in-service days being prepped by attorneys and bureaucrats about regulations and procedures—rather than working on improving their craft. Again, see the testimony of the Missouri special education director before Congress. Supportive of special education, she stated: *"The paperwork burden is fundamentally detracting from the education of students with disabilities."*[64]

What is stopping us from redirecting and transforming our system? Why the continued paralysis that keeps us from acting?

53

Where we need to be instead.

We need to redirect every piece of paper (including those over-the-top 30- to 40+-page IEPs), every meeting, and every procedure to one goal: does it lead to more learning and better teaching? If so, continue it. If not, end it.

We need to end the false security and comfort that in filling out all those pieces of paper and holding all those meetings, we somehow and improve student learning. Alas, we have no evidence to support that belief. A shift away from focusing on compliance to focusing on student outcomes will *not* be easy. For example, the Special Education Day Committee (SPEDCO) in Massachusetts responded to concerns about the paperwork burden in that state by developing an alternate process, Procedures Lite. Through it, parents and schools that work well together and have a history of successful implementation of an IEP can agree in writing to dispense with paperwork and procedures (always keeping the option of reverting to all the procedural requirements) and agree to simply work together for the child's benefit. While parties may be interested in pursuing this approach, they also seem to be reluctant to step away from the perceived safety of compliance with procedures and requirements—even when a more cooperative process might actually benefit the student and the relationship among them.[65]

It is time!

54

B. CHANGE THE PATH we are on.

We need to change the IDEA's direction and get on the right path. Let's keep our eye on the prize—that is, educating *all* students to high standards and preparing them for life after high school. The editors of *Rethinking Special Education for a New Century* conclude:

> *The choice confronting today's policymakers is not whether to keep the program as it is or return to the pre-IDEA status quo. Rather, the challenge is to modernize the program, **building on what we've learned about both special education and education in general.**[66]* (Emphasis added)

55

4. Educate all students, without labels. End reliance on the medical model as the gatekeeper for services.

To obtain special education services in the United States, a student needs to pass a gatekeeper to get a label signifying that she or he is diagnosed with one or more of the 14 disability categories. The term "medical model," as used here to describe that gatekeeper, denotes this system of diagnosis and prescription to "fix" or "treat" a disability. The law is based on the notion that something is wrong with the child that schools can fix or improve. Complicating the matter is that we often tend to pathologize behavior.[67]

Where we are now.

Consider that the law approaches labels as being rather fixed. In essence, we begin with the label to determine what students can or cannot do. Yet new brain research, suggests otherwise. See, for example, *Mindset: The New Psychology of Success*, by Stanford University's Carol Dweck.[68] Dweck focuses on two types of mindsets—fixed and growth. The *fixed mindset* assumes a person has certain intelligence and ability levels that determine his or her achievement and success.[69] The *growth mindset* assumes that a person learns continuously, accepts failure as part of learning, and grows beyond what may have initially been assumed by a label.

56

Consider the opportunity costs for children. What if, without labels, schools focused on skills and knowledge and practiced what students needed in order to learn? See, for example, *The Talent Code*, by Daniel Coyle.[70]

In short, some modern brain research about how children learn seems to contradict how we practice special education. Some of it even appears to defy the need for a labeling requirement for services. Some recent research questions whether there is a scientific basis for the notion of the "learning styles" approach that views students as either visual, auditory, or kinesthetic learners (VAK).[71] Could the research foundation of the special education system, too, be mired in 20th-century thinking?

The medical model raises other questions as well, including those related to the practice of conducting education according to political and social interest groups ("stakeholders"), not according to pedagogy. Thus, author and professor MaryAnn Byrnes, notes that *"special education is about the education of children who have a disability rather than those who struggle."*[72] **One set of kids has an entitlement; the other does not.** Why is that? And who can tell the difference between these groups? In *Rethinking Special Education*, G. Reid Lyon and colleagues delineate some of these issues:

> *Given what is now known about LD, it is irresponsible to continue current policies that dictate inadequate identification practices. . . . [F]rom its inception as a category, LD has served as a sociological sponge that attempts to wipe up general education's spills and cleanse its ills. . . . There are few areas where the relationship of science and policy are more loosely linked than LD.*[73]

57

Consider that we leave many children behind—simply because they have no label.[74] What if we just educated everyone? Although the "labeling business" might dry up, the "education business" might pick up!

Another troubling irony emerges from the gatekeeper system. By relying on labels, the IDEA may confuse general educators and let them off the hook from practicing good diagnostic and inclusive education. While undoubtedly most teachers work hard to educate all children in their classes, anecdotal evidence shows that some believe that students who do not have a label or an IEP do not need individual attention, extra support, accommodations, and so on. Could it be that labels get in the way of the natural tendency to teach all students in the class?[75]

58

Where we need to be instead.

We need to focus on educating *all* children—not on sorting and gatekeepers—and to provide services for students based on what they know and can do, not on *who* they are. Can they do the work? Do they need assistance? Are they way ahead? Way behind? Services, including early intervention and targeted assistance, should be based on students' current achievement, not on labels.[76] In this way, both "at risk" and advanced students can concentrate on material that challenges them.

Back in 2002, Steve Bartlett wrote in the report of the President's Commission on Excellence in Special Education, *"Services first, assessment later."*[77] And Don Asbridge, of the Kern Association of School Psychologists in California, wrote: *"Students need to go to school to get an education, not a diagnosis."*[78] **Yet here we still are.**

59

- The IDEA's and the NCLB's focus on response to intervention (RtI) appears to be a good start to move beyond the primacy of labels. RtI provides targeted assistance for young students, especially in reading and math. The theory is that if we teach children at their level, fewer of them will be referred for special education. Many labels will disappear. Issues about RtI—its efficacy and implementation—go far beyond this *little flipbook*.

- Consider, UNESCO's November 2008 conference, "Inclusive Education: The Way of the Future," which concluded that inclusive education is about *all* children, whoever and wherever they are, regardless of gender, ability, social status, disability, or language.[79] **SWD are part of the mix. Perhaps we can follow this path.**

- Every learning difference is not an illness or a defect. We are all different and learn differently. Teachers need to teach all types of learners with the many tools and tricks of the trade in their repertoire. Let that magic out.

It is time!

60

5. Change the role of parents in the law from "law enforcers" back to "parents."

We need to retool the IDEA's references to parents in two ways. First, the IDEA requires parents to enforce the law, to advocate for their children, and to battle the schools. In addition, the IDEA and the NCLB *detract* from and *undermine* parents' role as parents.

Where we are now.

The first role: parents as advocates who enforce the law. Relying on parents to enforce the law is problematic on many levels. For starters, it often destroys the relationship between school and home. It encourages schools to abandon their natural role as advocates for students. And it defies research; none supports this model as the "best practice" for enhancing teaching and learning.

Of course, parents respond to the legal mandates in many ways.

 **Some parents become hypervigilant,** hovering over their children's schooling excessively. These parents are often referred to as "helicopter parents."[80] Googling "in-service" and "helicopter parents" finds that some schools even provide in-service training programs for personnel to deal with the issues that hypervigilant parents present.

Other parents fret about their ability to carry out the burden placed on them.

61

In *Rethinking Special Education,* Tyce Palmaffy noted that advocates for the disabled *"worry about the regulatory burden being placed on parents":*

> *In a scathing indictment of federal enforcement efforts that was issued in January 2000, the National Council on Disability wrote, "Enforcement of the law is too often the burden of parents who must invoke formal complaint procedures and request due process hearings to obtain the services and supports to which their children are entitled under law." There is a powerful minority of parents who know their legal rights and aren't afraid to exercise them. But most parents are at a decided disadvantage vis-à-vis school administrators. They don't know their rights, have little experience with the legal system, and tend to respect the decisions of professional educators.[81]*

In upscale communities, perhaps it works. Parents there often can advocate, be persistent, and learn to play the system. Their children may be well served, perhaps overserved. It is an open secret that an SLD diagnosis often parallels zip codes and the SES (socioeconomic status) of the student's community. The system is skewed to affluent parents and to those who have the savvy and "pushiness" for "aggressively 'gaming' the system."[82]

62

When we factor in that many disability categories have fuzzy definitions, leading to great variations in the identification of SWD from city to city and state to state, we can envision the mass confusion and vast inequalities the broken system now fosters.

However, in many communities with lower SES, parents often cannot and usually do not take on that advocacy role—for many reasons. For example, some are not savvy about the process. Many parents trust what the schools are doing. Some don't have the resources to be advocates. Some don't understand the American system that rewards the squeaky wheel. As a result, their children are often underserved. Ironically, many of these children are needier.

The law creates incentives that are often perverse. Many parents now *want* their children to have a disability label. Why is that? They perceive that this is the only way their children can get individual attention. And, in fact, reliance on labels may, as discussed earlier, lead some educators to back away from providing the full panoply of options to students who have not been diagnosed and assigned a label.[83]

Relying on parents to fight against schools is unfair to them—and to everyone else. In this system, **the enforcement burden is inequitable and dysfunctional.**

63

The second role: detracting from the role of parents as parents.

The IDEA and the NCLB focus on parents as *consumers* in relation to their children's education. Under these laws, schools must provide parents with information about students, programs, teacher certifications, and so on. Parents are encouraged to demand services, seek alternate placements and tutoring, complain if a teacher is not "highly qualified," and so forth. In effect, these laws make parents bystanders to the education process—or demanding consumers. The laws fail to focus on the positive role parents can play in their children's education.

President Obama's exhortation to get parents to *partner* with schools and nurture their children is a far better approach:

> *There is no program and no policy that can substitute for a parent who is involved in their child's education from day one. There is no substitute for a parent who will make sure their children are in school on time and help them with their homework after dinner and attend those parent-teacher conferences. . . . And I have no doubt that we will still be talking about these problems in the next century if we do not have parents who are willing to turn off the TV once in a while and put away the video games and read to their child.*[84]

64

Of course, counter to what these laws emphasize and imply, the role of parents is *not* just to demand information, to file complaints, to be notified if their child's teacher is not "highly qualified," to demand a different school or tutoring, and so forth. Sure, those activities may be part of parenting, but they are hardly its essence.

The current laws' dysfunctional approach fosters disincentives for good parenting.

65

Where we need to be instead.

First, parents need to parent.

The laws should encourage that—not detract from this commonsense reality. We need to work together so that parents can help their children learn in school and can work with schools to improve learning.

Get the ball rolling by speaking and writing in plain language that parents can understand—not jargon, acronyms, and "edu-speak" that create intimidating barriers for parents. Many forces in the world are moving to "plain language."[85]

End the laws' silence on parenting. Provide "best practices" examples: what is helpful for parents to do, what is not, what is hyperparenting, what is appropriate. Create in-service training for educators *and* parents.

Get the incentives right. Engage parents to help students learn more and better.

Check out Bill Cosby and Dr. Alvin Poussaint's book, *Come On, People: On the Path from Victims to Victors.*[86] The authors provide practical examples to help parents parent. Poussaint suggested a national conference on parenting. Let's do it!

66

Refer again to President Obama's campaign speech on education, quoted earlier. Parents should turn off TVs and other ubiquitous technologies; should be present, not missing in action; and should support their children's education. **Schools can't educate students alone.**

Of course, the laws and schools can do only so much. Beyond abuse and neglect, a law cannot force parents to act in certain ways, nor can it micromanage their homes. Understood. However, laws, community leaders, politicians, and the media can be **powerful bully pulpits** to make the verb **"to parent"** *popular* and *potent* again.

For starters, we need to help parents to

1. Emphasize the importance of education and studying hard
2. Talk to their children (Research shows this to be the most important factor in school readiness.)[87]
3. Put them to bed early and feed them wholesome foods
4. Encourage them to be active learners and not do schoolwork for them
5. Support teachers and schools
6. Contribute to a positive learning community
7. Stop hovering

67

I recently visited a wonderful California public school that seems to do a great job. Excellent program. Fine teachers. Mission-driven for success. The school operates at full thrust. And yet the principal told our group of visitors, *"If I could only get the moms to put the children to bed early."*

There you have it.

Second, parents should not be the law's enforcers.

We need to amend the IDEA and NCLB messages and help parents move beyond their current advocacy and consumer roles to their parenting roles.

Let us lift the parents' burden to enforce the IDEA—a burden many do not want and should not have. Educators and schools can and should advocate for children. Is it possible that the rest of the world knows this already?

The 2008 report from UNESCO, cited above, recommends that its member states

> *promote school cultures and environments that are child-friendly, conducive to effective learning and inclusive of all children, healthy and protective, gender-responsive, and* ***encourage the active role and the participation of the learners themselves, their families and their communities.***[88]

It is time!

69

6. Treat inclusion as a means—not the end—of a good education.

Inclusion is the movement to educate SWD with general education standards and peers. The law states that SWD should be in the "least restrictive environment" (LRE, typically referring to regular programs and classrooms) "to the maximum extent appropriate." Of note, the law does not use the term "inclusion" or "full inclusion." It mandates appropriateness.

Where we are now.

The LRE requirement has been confusing and not always focused on teaching and learning. Education should be about student outcomes and achievement and preparing students for their future lives, not about popular catchphrases, just passing tests, or having SWD sit in mainstream classes to placate some adults' views of how schools should be.

Too often, however, inclusion has crossed the line and become the end, not the means.[89] The Principals' Partnership has stated, *"According to the literature, inclusion is not a strategy, but a philosophy."*[90]

With all due respect, philosophy is misplaced here, especially when it does not track (and often contradicts) good teaching practices and learning.[91]

70

A bit of history. How did we get here? Following *Brown v. Board of Education of Topeka*, the landmark 1954 racial discrimination lawsuit, the notion of educating SWD in regular schools emerged.[92] *Separate is not equal.* Remember? Inclusion grew out of the civil rights movement, not out of research-based approaches or best practices. It was pushed by advocates who argued that, to learn and become self-sufficient, SWD needed to be educated among nondisabled peers. Courts often based education-related rulings on the equal protection and due process clauses of the Fourteenth Amendment, not on sound teaching practices.

71

The public sometimes gets it before the politicians do. Note the following survey results frpm the 36th Annual Phi Beta Kappa Gallup Poll of the Public's Attitudes Towards the Public Schools:

> *The public does not support . . . the inclusion of special education students on the same basis as all other students. . . . The data . . . indicate that the public rejects holding special education students to the same grade-level standards as other students [and] rejects their inclusion in the base for determining if a school is in need of improvement. . . . This issue may prove difficult to resolve, since many in the special education community believe special education students should be included and judged according to the same standards as all other students.*[93]

Belief systems are powerful. They often rule. Yet ask yourself, why are so many special education disputes about parents trying to remove children from inclusive settings to private schools or separate classes, where the children will be with *only* other SWD?[94]

Learning and teaching are based on hard work, not on whether students sit in inclusive or separate classrooms. Lawyers, judges, politicians, and lobbyists do *not* teach children. Teachers do. It's time to let teachers do just that—in the way and the place that works well for all students.

72

Where we need to be instead.

- **Base inclusion on educational, not political, criteria.** See James M. Kauffman and Daniel P. Hallahan's book, *The Illusion of Full Inclusion: A Comprehensive Critique of a Current Special Education Bandwagon.*[95]

- **Focus on pedagogy** (*how* to teach different learners) and **improve the quality of teaching.** See *The Teaching Gap*, a wonderful (and short) book that compares math teaching practices in the United States, Japan, and Germany.[96]

- **Follow civil rights goals and mottoes when they are consistent with best teaching practices.** There's a place for every belief and assertion of a "right," but that place is not always in our nation's inclusive classrooms.

Pedagogy—not philosophy—should control.

It is time!

73

7. Focus on the WHOLE child—strengths as well as weaknesses.

I ask audiences, "How many of you became as successful as you are in your chosen career by focusing only on what you *cannot* do?" *No one* ever raises a hand.

Yet in special education we endlessly splice and dice weaknesses and diagnoses. The law mentions, but does not emphasize, student strengths. As a result, we have inadvertently created a generation of SWD who focus on what they *cannot* do.

Where we are now.

When I meet a young person who introduces himself with, "Hi. I'm John. I'm learning disabled," I fear the battle is lost. Why is that the child's lead descriptor? Or how about the child who says he can't do something because he is learning disabled? The label precedes the result.

74

I vividly recall when I was a hearing officer, listening to a mother testify about her son and all that he could not do. She cited endless evidence, test scores, and so on. I surprised her by asking, "Do you like this person? Is there anything he *can* do?" She lightened up noticeably and smiled. She had focused only on the negative, not the positive. Sad, isn't it, how the law is at work?

Psychologists Robert J. Sternberg and Elena L. Grigorenko ask, *"How could we have started down the path of encouraging people to capitalize on their weaknesses rather than their strengths? As is often the case, the goal was noble—to ensure that students with learning disabilities received the kind of education to which they were entitled. . . . Along the way, though, some things began to go wrong. . . . [W]hat began as a quest for justice became perceived by some people as an entitlement."*[97]

Schools hire many outside diagnosticians who focus on weaknesses in children. Of course, many teachers are seekers and promoters of strengths. But schools hire far fewer outside professionals who are strength seekers, and the law often impedes teachers' efforts to enhance student strengths. It's time to let them at it.[98]

The current approach cannot have a happy ending. We should rethink the law's approach that seems to elevate the label above effort, and weakness above strength.

75

Where we need to be instead.

• **Let's learn from the business community.** Best-seller lists are filled with books focusing on people's strengths. A few examples:

• **Marcus Buckingham**'s *Now, Discover Your Strengths* [99]

• **Tom Rath**'s *The Truth about You*

• **Paul Orfalea**, founder of Kinko's, has learning disabilities and ADD. In *Copy This! Lessons from a Hyperactive Dyslexic Who Turned a Bright Idea into One of America's Best Companies*, he describes how he learned that his "deficits" were the root of his innovation and achievement. He shares this trait with many other successful people, including Leonardo da Vinci, Winston Churchill, Albert Einstein, Walt Disney, Richard Branson (Virgin Airlines and Virgin Records), Craig McCaw (telecom pioneer), John Chambers (Cisco), and Charles Schwab. Here are a few of this thoughts:

> *I'm in good company. All of these innovators survived an educational system determined to make them feel like failures. We are the lucky ones.*

> *When tearful parents come up to me to talk about their child's "learning disorder," I ask them, "Oh, you mean his learning opportunity? What is your child good at? What does he like to do?" When I meet kids, I tell them, "You are blessed." It is easy to forget that part of the equation in the face of a dire-sounding prognosis.* [100]

• **Capitalize on children's strengths.** Bring in vocational counselors, recruiters, entrepreneurs, admissions officers, and others who look for what young people *can* do. What good is served by building on weakness?

76

- Vocational technical high schools seem to get it. The Pioneer Institute in Massachusetts released a 2008 study of vocational schools that found student achievement generally high, especially for SWD. This is so even though these schools have a higher percentage of SWD than regular high schools. Why the success? Could it be because students focus on what they can and like to do (computer repair, automotive repair, beautician services, etc.) as well as on what is hard (academics)? Strengths help overcome weaknesses.[101]

- Joe Lamacchia and Bridget Samburg's book, *Blue Collar and Proud of It*, and Matthew B. Crawford's article "The Case for Working with Your Hands" are excellent reads.[102] Hopefully, we are in the midst of a societal change . . . a change that has perhaps been prompted by the economic downturn.

- Teaching through student strengths helps SWD learn, even in their areas of weaknesses. Active learning—project-based and real-world learning experience—combined with academics and other requirements, seems to work for many students. We need a more strengths-based approach to teaching and learning.

- Focusing on strengths confirms that there are many paths for success.[103] What is so special about a one-size-fits-all approach?

It is time!

77

8. Remind students, parents, and teachers that education is an active process.

Although education is an *active* process, the IDEA and the NCLB focus on what schools do *for* students. Under the NCLB, if students don't progress, their schools can be sanctioned. Under the IDEA, parents can *sue* schools.

Instead of focusing on SWD as active participants in their own education, even (and especially) when the going gets tough, these laws invest parents and students with "rights" and place accountability for learning with others.

Does that make sense? No. It also made no sense to Albert Shanker, the head of the American Federation of Teachers and an influential and inspiring leader of our time.

In discussing the proposed NCLB (back in 1994) in his weekly *New York Times* column, Where We Stand, he wrote, *"Imagine saying we should shut down a hospital and fire its staff because not all of its patients became healthy."* [104] His closing lines:

> *Students won't learn more unless they work harder—come to school, pay attention and do homework. But they are unlikely to work harder when they've been told that if they don't, their teachers will be punished. There is no school system that works this way and I doubt that any ever will, at least not successfully.*

78

Where we are now.

- We have lost our way many times in the last 30-plus years.

- We lower standards and dumb down requirements. Secretary of Education Arne Duncan is blunt: we need to stop lying to parents and students.

- Our laws do not emphasize resiliency—helping students overcome hardships and challenges—as a growth process. Too often these laws invoke the blame game when students do not succeed.

- Even truancy policies too often seem to be upside down, faulting schools for truancy by SWD even when a student's disability is unrelated to his or her failure to attend school.

79

Good public policy? Good life lessons? Good law? Good research-based approach? No! No! No! And no!

Consider some popular books. While they don't focus on SWD, perhaps it's time to amend the education laws' thrust away from blaming others to focusing on student effort and achievement. Daniel Coyle's *Talent Code* emphasizes the importance of hard work and practice—building myelin in our brains. In the spirit of the aphorism that practice makes perfect, he writes, *"Practice makes myelin."*[105]

Consider Malcolm Caldwell's best seller *Outliers*, with its message about individual grit and the 10,000-hour rule: to get good at something, you need to put in 10,000 hours of work at it.

Consider Jonah Lehrer's article "The Truth about Grit," which cites Carol Dweck's work and emphasizes the importance of old-fashioned values of showing up, not giving up, and working hard to achieve success.[106]

Common sense tells us that there is no substitute for active participation in our learning. And, of course, many SWD work hard and give it 100%. Yet the law continues to place the accountability burden elsewhere. Lowering standards and blaming schools won't cut it.

Common sense. Everyone knows such things, but these laws don't reflect that knowledge. The incentive system they create is backward.

80

Where we should be instead.

- We should rethink the accountability we place on schools when students (and parents) don't do their part. We should train for responsibility and accountability—by students—as well as schools.

- We need to focus on children as active learners to help them succeed. And, yes, to help them learn to work hard when necessary and to be resilient.[107]

- Examples from other countries that focus on active learning may be useful. *The Learning Gap* compares American students to their peers in Japan and China. In the United States, parents, teachers, and students often assume that success and failure are based on a student's innate ability or disability. In contrast, Asians refer to environmental factors and the students' own efforts to explain school performance.[108] It's the difference between a *fixed mindset* and a *growth mindset*, as discussed above.

- The 2008 UNESCO report on inclusive education, mentioned above, encourages *"the active role and the participation of the learners themselves, their families and their communities."*[109]

81

- We need to end the IDEA's silence so that students are incentivized to be active participants in their own education. Schools cannot do it alone.

- Finally, let's honor some heroes with disabilities who overcame adversity and achieved great success, such as Orfalea, Schwab, Branson, and Einstein.

It is time!

9. End the overuse of accommodations. Stop lying to students, parents, and regulators.

Accommodations may mask a student's lack of skills and knowledge and/or provide an unfair advantage to SWD.

Too often, we forget what accommodations are supposed to do—and *not* do. They are supposed to provide access and learning opportunities for SWD. Accommodations are *changes* in materials, programs, settings, and so on that SWD *need* in order to *access* them and that *do not fundamentally alter or lower* standards, requirements, or expectations. In testing, they do not change the test construct.

Where we are now.

Accommodations are not supposed to make work easier, give an advantage, raise scores, or help students pass. As a 2004 *Phi Delta Kappan* article reminds us, special education and accommodations are designed to *enable* students to learn, not to *disable* them.[110]

Modifications are different. They *do* fundamentally alter standards and constructs, usually lowering standards or expectations. While the work may be challenging for the student, its level of difficulty is less complex and at a lower level than the classroom standards or test constructs.[111]

To establish standards, educators and test makers need to articulate *what* they are teaching, measuring, and valuing. Clarity is key in these policy choices.

Having high standards is *not* unlawful discrimination.

83

When it comes to accommodations, **we have created a mess.** Accommodations are often viewed as a right.[112] And too often they do lower standards, confuse the special education world, and distort the truth without providing appropriate notice to citizens, parents, students, and others.[113]

According to the IDEA, special education is designed to *"prepare [children with disabilities] for further education, employment, and independent living."*[114] Yet, too often, educators are pressured to provide accommodations and to "pass" students, no matter what. Thus SWD may have "accommodations" (really modifications)—without transparency. Again, that is *not* the purpose of accommodations. And how exactly does this tactic help SWD learn and prepare for life?

For example, IEPs may provide elementary school students who have not learned to read with someone to read to them. We must ask: For what purpose? **What is "special" about not learning to read?** Of course, there may be some students for whom that service is appropriate, and in those cases, notice to parents and others must be clear—that is, the accommodation has the "side effect" of not focusing on teaching the student how to read.

A recent notice at SpecialEdAdvocate.org, a parent advocacy group, stated: *"Many parents have concerns about their child's reading performance, but are getting mixed messages from schools and inflated report cards."*[115]

So sad and so wrong. Who is helped by inflated reports?

We must ask: Is it right to raise children for a lifetime of accommodations—instead of accomplishment and skills? Is it right to provide a watered-down curriculum to get children "through"? Focusing on "passing" all students is a distortion if done by lowering standards and providing too many invalidating accommodations.[116] Psychologists Robert J. Sternberg and Elena L. Grigorenko point out:

> *The irony is that U.S. society may be hurting rather than helping students with LDs. The society may be giving these children false expectations, when in fact it does not continue to provide after the school years the crutches that it provides during these years.*[117]

85

Where we should be instead.

- **We need to stop lying to SWD and parents.** In discussing school standards for all students, Secretary of Education Arne Duncan stated that *"we have to stop lying to children . . . and stop 'dumbing down' and lowering standards in so many places."*[118]

- Educators, students, and parents need to have that difficult conversation:

  - Some students will *not* pass that exam and will not earn a diploma.
  - Some students may need more than four years to earn a diploma.
  - IEPs should not cover up failure due to lack of skills or knowledge by incorporating too many accommodations.
  - Schools should teach coping and compensatory strategies.

An unpublished 2005 Third Circuit Court of Appeals decision faulted a New Jersey school for overstating a fourth-grade student's actual progress by providing too many accommodations. The court found that, in an effort to boost the student's self-esteem, the district had based grades on effort, not achievement, and had provided many accommodations. The student's passing grades did not reflect his achievement.[119]

86

- Schools need to provide fewer accommodations and to focus on teaching and learning. Happily, the RtI (response to intervention) approach in general education classrooms is heading in that direction.

- As well, it is good news that many researchers and the US ED are revisiting NCLB's insistence that *all* children meet the same standards. If accountability assessments continue, the move to "value-added" scoring and reporting should lead to a more transparent and better solution.

- In an article titled "Time to Kill 'No Child Left Behind,'" American education historian Diane Ravitch wrote: *"The worst part of the law is its unrealistic demand that all students must be proficient by 2014. No other nation and no state has ever reached this unrealistic goal. Every educator knows that it is impossible."* [120]

- Again, Albert Shanker adds to the discussion:

  The next time anyone is inclined to sneer at the basics as "traditional," I suggest he or she visit with a 12th or even 6th grader who can barely read, write, or compute and look at the pain and frustration on that student's face. [121]

It is time!

87

C. REBALANCE SCHOOLS for all students.

We need to change direction away from the IDEA's 20th-century procedures and legal requirements about processes and providing services (inputs) to a 21st-century approach that focuses on the outcomes and results for student learning.

The law's excesses must be curbed. Too much of a good thing is a bad thing.

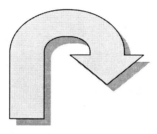

88

10. Curb excesses in the law. Educate ALL students, starting from where they currently function.

The oft-repeated slogan "All means all" belies what actually happens in our educational system. The truism does not ring true. Rather, schools focus more attention and funds on some students than others.

A recent *CommonWealth Magazine* study of the tug-of-war between special and general education pointed out that school budgets are being cut—but not in special education. One school superintendent asked, *"How do you set up a class of human beings who are entitled to an education [while] everyone else gets what's left over?"*[122]

Where we are.

As discussed earlier, SWD have an entitlement for services. All other students do not—whether they are average, at-risk, advanced (e.g., gifted and talented), non–English speakers, or bored. Unfortunately, too often schools do not provide non-SWD with the same level of focus, funding, or effort.

The word "special" has led us astray—the reality is that all children are unique and need appropriate educational services.[123] But in the current broken system, who will tell the others that they are not protected, are not special, and do not deserve appropriate services?[124]

89

In many troubling ways, this law, as it moves into the realm of unintended consequences and dysfunction, is no longer fair to others or to the common good. It makes no sense in today's inclusive world.

Is it fair? Students with a disability **label** receive more services than others (whether low, average, or high achievers) who also need extra help. Tyce Palmaffy observes, *"The question of why learning disabled children are more deserving of extra help than everyday low achievers is one that LD advocates have never quite answered."*[125]

Is it fair? Schools and states expend inordinate effort to get SWD (and other "gap students") to pass tests for NCLB accountability. The law requires *all* students to be proficient and leads to vast inconsistencies in how schools work with different groups of students.

Is it fair? Only SWD receive **transition planning** to help prepare them for life beyond high school. Many students who enter college drop out. Some return home, unable to find or hold a job. The tagline "They Just Won't Grow Up" for *Time*'s cover story "Meet the Twixters" tells the tale. Some call this new phenomenon a "failure to launch."[126] These young adults are on their own, with no entitlement or legal claim.

90

Is it fair? Often, **disruptive students** (including SWD who have additional rights) remain in classes, even as they hinder the learning of others. Indeed, recent research shows that one disruptive student impedes the learning for all—the "bad apple' peer-effect model.[127]

This commonsense reality is well known but is often swept under the rug by legalistic policies created in Washington, D.C. What happened to the opportunity for classmates to learn? And what is happening to our nation's supply of well-educated young people when disruptions and interruptions prevent students from focusing in the classroom. These students have no rights or entitlements. Sad but true.

Is it fair? Only students with disabilities continue to receive educational services after being **expelled.** The others? They get to stand on street corners.

Stanford professor Mark Kelman writes: *"We should scrutinize all claims that non-disabled students face disruption. . . . But we should be equally wary of a system that forbids us from counting the educational interests of 'mainstream' students just as worthy as those of pupils with disabilities."*[128]

91

Is it fair? At-risk students fall through the cracks. Austin, Texas, attorney Jim Walsh calls these students **WBFWR** (Way Behind for Whatever Reason). They have no entitlements to services. While an SLD student gets a FAPE, a slow reader (for whatever reason) gets little. One irony is that many educators and evaluators can't tell the difference between these groups of students.[129] Those fuzzy eligibility criteria at work!

Again, Professor Kelman notes: *"In a world of limited resources, it is plainly not enough to say that children with learning disabilities 'deserve' more resources; their claims inevitably compete with claims that could be made for other 'deserving' pupils who can be described in a wide variety of ways (such as poor achievers, socioeconomically disadvantaged, and gifted but understimulated)."*

Kelman concludes, *"Until we see that these are important education issues but not civil rights claims, we will not make rational policy in this area."*[130]

Is it fair? Some SWD take the **SAT** or **ACT** with extended time, yet the score reports sent to schools and colleges do not indicate these altered conditions.[131] What about other students who find tests stressful and would benefit from more time? And what about the effect of this practice on the validity of these very test results for all students applying to college?

These are but a few examples of how this law of good intentions has moved beyond providing access and opportunity for SWD, to skewing the playing field and providing unfair advantages to some—but not to *all* students.

Alas, "all" does not mean all. Rights for only some create unintended negative consequences for others.

93

Where we need to be instead.

So, what can we do?

Study the value-added approach to assessments that measures the improvement made by various groups—not just whether the groups meet a specific target score. Piloted in several states, it shows promise. Let's find out what value the teachers and students added to the achievement and how much progress *all* students, including SWD, actually make.

End the confusion that having standards is somehow discriminatory. It is *not*. It is not unlawful to set high standards, even if some students can't meet them and even if the reason is due to their disability.[132]

Consider basketball. Some of us are short. Should baskets be lowered for some players? If that were done, would it still be basketball?

94

Confront the unfairness of accommodations (as on the SAT and ACT), student discipline procedures (which lead SWD to a FAPE and others to street corners), transition planning for only some, and so forth. We need to focus on *all* students and ask whether programs are fair and in the public interest. If not, we should end these preferences that have morphed over time to become examples of good intentions gone awry. As for the SAT and ACT, since some students already have extended time and the College Board (which administers the SAT) and the ACT provide *no* notice to colleges and schools of that altered condition, why do they not just extend that benefit to all students? Given the current ACT and SAT practice, we can infer that the test makers don't really believe that the length of time is a necessary and material condition. So why all the fuss?

- **Pay more than lip service to the rest of our students** and, in particular, to advanced students who need academic stimulation. Our country needs for them to meet their potential. Yet, worrisome new recent research shows they are not holding their own, leading to an **international achievement gap.**[133]

- **Prepare students for college.** Having them attend college, only to get remediation, is a black eye on our system. Having them attend, only to drop out, is unsustainable bad public policy. Having our top students not perform up to par is the most troubling. We need to rebalance our priorities.

- **Everyone is special.** All means all. It is in our nation's interest to educate *all* students to their highest possible achievement levels. Pure and simple.

- Google got it right: *"Focus on the user. The rest will follow."* We need to get back to that truism. Every student needs our focused attention.

It is time!

95

11. Follow the money for special education and educating SWD—a most challenging endeavor.

Oops! We can't really follow the money. We don't actually know how much we spend of local, state, and federal dollars to educate students with disabilities—or where it is going.

Books and research reports have been written about this challenge; here, but a few words.

Where we are now.

After more than 35 years, we still don't have good data. National expenditures on special education are not well tracked, even though we know that they are rising faster than expenditures for general education.[134] In 2002, estimates were that we spent some $80 billion annually on IDEA services, but a clear accounting has not been made.[135] How much do we spend on teaching and learning? On paperwork? On litigation? On services in general education classrooms for SWD, including the widespread use of one-on-one aides? On waste or fraud? On various disability categories? How much is spent in each state?

96

We seem to have moved from a public good to overwhelming fiscal needs that cannot be controlled by school districts or states. It is not clear how the additional $12 billion in federal stimulus funds will be spent or how effective it will be at improving learning by SWD.

Despite all we do know, nothing really changes. The courts continue to rule that lack of funding is not a defense for schools or states. Special education is an entitlement in their eyes, and schools need to spend whatever it takes to provide a FAPE.

A sad reality is that we are not even sure if our money is well spent. Consider this from the spring 2009 issue of *CommonWealth Magazine*: *"The cost of special education in Massachusetts is approaching $2 billion a year.... There is little evidence that the state's ... investment is paying off as hoped."*[136]

97

Where we need to be instead.

- Before we throw new money at special education, we need a transformation.
- We need to know where the money is spent. Separate the costs for programs in both general education and special education settings, for bureaucracy, and for litigation.
- Taxpayers have a right to know the real costs—in plain English. Perhaps this knowledge will shock us out of our complacency and our old categorical spending model.

While we pay lip service to the need to compete against the best students in other countries, we continue our 20th-century funding structure. The authors of *Genius Denied: How to Stop Wasting Our Brightest Young Minds* note that *"America spends 143 times more on special education than gifted education."*[137] In early 2009, President Obama told Congress that a decline in education outcomes relative to other countries *"is a prescription for economic decline, because we know the countries that out-teach us today will out-compete us tomorrow."*[138] In the meantime, the international achievement gap continues.

It is time to focus our energy and resources on *all* students. We have no conclusive evidence that continuing to spend 20% to 40% of school budgets on special education and IEPs for SWD is truly the best way to teach them. We have no definitive data that this is the best allocation of resources to prepare us to compete in the global economy. Rather, this policy seems to be held in place by inertia, the pull of political correctness, and fear of systemic reform.

It is time!

98

12. **Create an action plan.**

The final step for reform of our education system is to create an **action plan** to start the transformation. Together we can and must do the following:

- **Allow open discussions about reform** of our broken special education system.
- **Convene a wide array of stakeholders**—general and special educators, parents of general and special education students, students (both general and regular education), businesspeople, taxpayers, and policymakers—to build real systemwide reform.
- **Hold a national conference about parenting,** as Dr. Alvin Poussaint suggested.[139]
- **Expand efforts to keep what's working and change what's not.**[140]
- **Give voice to what many folks already know: our broken system needs to be fixed.** In writing this book I was struck by the encouragement from so many different people. They all know we have a problem that needs a solution—and needs it now. Again, as President Obama put it:

    It is time for us to act on what everyone knows to be true.

- **Get real, and deal with the elephant in the room—finally.**

99

The Vision

Let's keep our eye on the prize:

- Educating *all* children, including SWD, to appropriately high standards.
- Meeting America's challenges in the world through education.
- Creating policies that are fair and equitable and make sense for America in the 21st century.

Reform does *not* seek to or allow us to go back to 20th-century exclusions. Those days are gone forever. We won the access civil rights–era battles. Going backward is a false and paralyzing choice. It is *not* on the table, nor should it be. We live in an inclusive world now.

100

Let us work together with creativity and boldness.

- Let us move beyond the IDEA's historic success. We need mission change, not continued mission creep. Inertia, fear, and the same old same old should not continue to rule. We need to question assumptions and have the courage to change the way "we've always done it" for almost 35 years.
- Let us end the reality that, in many damaging ways, schools that try to move forward are hindered by the "can't touch" status of this law.

Together, let us focus attention and resources on research and teaching for *all* students. Everything else will follow.

Let the transformative winds of change blow freely!

101

Timeline of Cases and Laws

Please refer to the list of acronyms and terms on page vii.

1954   *Brown v. Board of Education* (Supreme Court decision about segregated schools: separate is not equal.)
1972   *Pennsylvania Association of Retarded Citizens (PARC) v. Commonwealth of Pennsylvania*
1972   *Mills v. Board of Education of the District of Columbia* (The two 1972 district court decisions led to the end of the exclusion of many SWD from public schools.)
1973   Section 504 of the Rehabilitation Act of 1973
1975   EAHCA or EHA, now called the IDEA
1975   *Goss v. Lopez* (Due process rights for students in schools)
1982   *Board of Education of the Hendrick Hudson School District v. Rowley* (Supreme Court analysis of a free appropriate public education, or FAPE)
1986   Precursor law to the IDEA, allowed for reimbursement for parents of their attorneys' fees in special education hearings, with some conditions.
1990   ADA
1997   The special education law renamed as the IDEA—the Individuals with Disabilities Education Act (The law includes the requirement that SWD participate in the "general curriculum" to the maximum extent appropriate.)
2002   NCLB
2004   IDEA reauthorization; statute renamed the Individuals with Disabilities Education Improvement Act (The IDEA provides that, under some conditions, schools can seek attorneys' fees from parents.)
2005   *Schaffer v. Weast* (Burden-of-proof case)
2009   ADAA
2009   *Forest Grove School District v. T.A.* (Private school reimbursement case)

Suggested Recources

As I benefited greatly from many of these books by today's thought leaders, I share them with you.

Buckingham, Marcus, and Donald O. Clifton. *Now, Discover Your Strengths.* New York: Free Press, 2001.

Byrnes, MaryAnn. *Taking Sides: Clashing Views in Special Education.* 4th ed. Boston: McGraw-Hill Higher Education, 2009.

Cosby, Bill, and Alvin F. Poussaint, M.D. *Come On, People: On the Path from Victims to Victors.* Nashville, TN: Thomas Nelson, 2007.

Covey, Stephen M. R. *The Speed of Trust: The One Thing That Changes Everything.* New York: Free Press, 2006.

Coyle, Daniel. *The Talent Code: Greatness Isn't Born. It's Grown. Here's How.* New York: Bantam Books, 2009.

Dweck, Carol S. *Mindset: The New Psychology of Success.* New York: Ballantine Books, 2006.

Education Week. *The Obama Education Plan: An Education Week Guide.* San Francisco: Jossey-Bass, 2009.

Finn, Chester E., Jr., Andrew J. Rotherham, and Charles R. Hokanson Jr., eds. *Rethinking Special Education for a New Century.* Washington, DC: Thomas B. Fordham Foundation and the Progressive Policy Institute, 2001.

Freedman, Miriam Kurtzig. *Student Testing and the Law* (to be republished in 2009); *Grades, Report Cards, Etc. . . . and the Law* (2008); *IEP and Section 504 Team Meetings . . . and the Law* (2008). School Law Pro, www.schoollawpro.com.

Glendon, Mary Ann. *Rights Talk: The Impoverishment of Political Discourse.* New York: Free Press, 1991.

Hanushek, Eric A., and Alfred L. Lindseth. *Schoolhouses, Courthouses, and Statehouses: Solving the Funding-Achievement Puzzle in America's Public Schools.* Princeton, NJ: Princeton University Press, 2009.

Hehir, Thomas, and Thomas Latus. *Special Education at the Century's End.* Cambridge, MA: Harvard Educational Review, 1992.

Howard, Philip K. *The Death of Common Sense.* New York: Random House, 1994.

———. *Life without Lawyers: Liberating Americans from Too Much Law.* New York: W. W. Norton, 2009.

Kahlenberg, Richard D. *Tough Liberal: Albert Shanker and the Battle over Schools, Unions, Race, and Democracy.* New York: Columbia University Press, 2007.

Lamacchia, Joe, and Bridget Samburg. *Blue Collar and Proud of It: The All-in-One Resource for Finding Freedom, Financial Success, and Security outside the Cubicle.* Deerfield Beach, FL: Health Communications, 2009.

Levitt, Steven D., and Stephen J. Dubner. *Freakonomics: A Rogue Economist Explores the Hidden Side of Everything.* New York: William Morrow, 2005.

Orfalea, Paul. *Copy This! Lessons from a Hyperactive Dyslexic Who Turned a Bright Idea into One of America's Best Companies.* New York: Workman, 2005.

President's Commission on Excellence in Special Education. *A New Era: Revitalizing Special Education for Children and Their Families.* Washington, DC, 2002.

Sommers, Christina Hoff, and Sally Satel, M.D. *One Nation under Therapy: How the Helping Culture Is Eroding Self-Reliance.* New York: St. Martin's Press, 2005.

Sternberg, Robert J., and Elena L. Grigorenko. *Our Labeled Children.* Cambridge, MA: Perseus, 1999.

Stevenson, Harold W., and James W. Stigler. *The Learning Gap.* New York: Simon and Schuster, 1992.

Yell, Mitchell L. *The Law and Special Education.* Upper Saddle River, NJ: Merrill/Prentice Hall, 1998.

Notes

1. The EHA, or EAHCA, is the Education for All Handicapped Children Act; the IDEA is the Individuals with Disabilities Education Improvement Act, 20 USC 1400 et seq.

2. *Pennsylvania Association of Retarded Children (PARC) v. Commonwealth of Pennsylvania*, 343 F. Supp. 279 (E.D.Pa. 1972); and *Mills v. Board of Education of District of Columbia*, 348 F. Supp. 866 (D.D.C. 1972).

3. Erin Dillon, "Labeled: The Students behind NCLB's 'Disabilities' Designation" (July 2007), Education Sector, www.educationsector.org/analysis/analysis_show.htm?doc_id=509392.

4. Perry A. Zirkel, "The Over-Legalization of Special Education," *West's Education Law Reporter* 195 (March 24, 2005): 35, citing the President's Commission on Excellence in Special Education, *A New Era: Revitalizing Special Education for Children and Their Families* (Washington, DC, 2002).

5. Dillon, "Labeled," 12.

6. Chester E. Finn Jr., Andrew J. Rotherham, and Charles R. Hokanson Jr., eds., summary of chapter 2, "Time to Make Special Education 'Special' Again," by Wade F. Horn and Douglas Tynan, in *Rethinking Special Education for a New Century* (Washington, DC: Thomas B. Fordham Foundation and the Progressive Policy Institute, 2001), www.ppionline.org/ndol/print.cfm?contentid=3344.

7. President's Commission, *A New Era*, www.ed.gov/inits/commissionsboards/whspecialeducation/index.html, 3.

8. See, e.g., Bruce Mohl and Jack Sullivan, "Isn't Every Child Special?" *CommonWealth Magazine*, Spring 2009, www.massinc.org.

9. Some might argue this law was designed for more than resolving exclusion of students from schooling. But it is clear that these early cases and law point to the access issue as the primary impediment for SWD at the time (1970s).

10. Some would say we need to end special education and its labeling of children per se and just educate children. See, e.g., Donald J. Asbridge, "Top 17: State and Federal Educational Programs That Need to Go . . . ," in "Does It Work?" an open letter to President Obama (n.d.), www.kernschoolpsych.org/febkog28.htm. Dr. Asbridge is a school psychologist and the editor of *KOG* (*KASP Online Gazette*). And see Kevin P. Dwyer (NCSP, past NASP president, and recipient of the NASP Lifetime Achievement Award), "'Rights without Labels': Words or Actions?" *NASP Communiqué* (November 2006), www.nasponline.org/publications/cq/pdf/cqNov06.pdf.

11. Philip K. Howard, *Life without Lawyers: Liberating Americans from Too Much Law* (New York: W. W. Norton, 2009; www.lifewithoutlawyers.com), 14.

12. As enacted, S. 6, approved November 29, 1975, is Public Law 94-142 (89 Stat. 773).

13. A few of us were so moved by this signing statement that we launched an annual national holiday on December

2, Special Education Day, to mark the occasion. It celebrates successes in special education and promotes systemic reform in going forward. For more information, visit www.specialeducationday.com.

14. Anthony Lewis, review of *Life without Lawyers*, by Philip K. Howard, *New York Review of Books*, April 9, 2009.

15. Professor Bill Koski, Stanford Law School, pers. comm., 2009.

16. President's Commission, *A New Era*, 16.

17. Ibid., 11, 12, 17.

18. *Webster's Ninth New Collegiate Dictionary* (1988).

19. Special education has been faulted as a "wait to fail" model. That is, only if a student is far behind might he or she be eligible for special education services. See, e.g., G. Reid Lyon, Jack M. Fletcher, Sally E. Shaywitz, Bennett A. Shaywitz, Joseph K. Torgesen, Frank B. Wood, Ann Schulte, and Richard Olson, "Rethinking Learning Disabilities," in Finn et al., *Rethinking Special Education*, 266, 269. Note that the movement to RtI (Response to Intervention) is a direct response to the "wait to fail" approach. Hopefully, we will teach students how to read, do math, and understand science so that they will not fall behind and require special education.

20. MaryAnn Byrnes, *Taking Sides: Clashing Views in Special Education*, 4th ed. (New York: McGraw-Hill Higher Education, 2009), Issue 7.

21. Madeleine Will, testimony at "Improving NCLB: Successes, Concerns, Solutions," Commission on No Child Left Behind hearing, September 25, 2006, www.aspeninstitute.org.

22. Quoted by Linda Darling-Hammond, presentation at Commonwealth Club, San Francisco, July 8, 2009.

23. For a thoughtful, cogent discussion of the need for a "unified system of education" for all students, see Kim Goodrich Ratcliffe and David T. Willard, "NCLBA and IDEA: Perspectives from the Field," *Focus on Exceptional Children* 30, no. 3 (November 2006).

24. Ibid.

25. Many studies bear this out, including American Association for Research, *Educating Students with Disabilities: Comparing Methods for Explaining Expenditure Variation*, Special Education Expenditure Project, Report 7 (Office of Special Education Programs, U.S. Department of Education, May 2004), www.csef-air.org/publications/seep/national/Rpt7.PDF; and Stephen Lipscomb, *Students with Disabilities and California's Special Education Program* (2009), Public Policy Institute of California (PPIC) report, www.ppic.org.

26. See "Who Pays for Special Ed?" *Time*, September 25, 2006.

27. See, e.g., studies by the Center for Special Education Finance, www.csef-air.org.

28. Mohl and Sullivan, "Isn't Every Child Special?"

29. See Finn et al., *Rethinking Special Education*; and research by the Massachusetts Association of School Superintendents, www.massupt.org.

30. *"In 1999–2000, schools in the U.S. were spending an average of $6,556 to educate a student without disabilities. At the same time, schools were spending an average of $12,639 on each student eligible for special education."* Jay G. Chambers, Maria Perez, Miguel Socias, Jamie Shkolnik, and Phil Esra, *Educating Students with Disabilities: Comparing Methods for Explaining Expenditure Variations*, Special Education Expenditure Project, Report 7 (American Institutes for Research, May 2004), 5.

31. Stanley M. Elam, Lowell C. Rose, and Alec M. Gallup, "The 28th Annual Phi Delta Kappa/Gallup Poll of the Public's Attitudes toward the Public Schools," *Phi Delta Kappan* 78 (1996). See similar findings in Ericha Parks, "Special Education Funding, or Lack Thereof, Forces School Districts to Suffer," *Houston Examiner.com*, May 13, 2009, www.examiner.com.

32. *26th Annual Report to Congress on the Implementation of the Individuals with Disabilities Education Act, 2004*, vol. 2 (Washington, DC: Office of Special Education and Rehabilitative Services, U.S. Department of Education, 2006), www.ed.gov/about/reports/annual/osep/2004/26th-vol-2.pdf, 36.

33. President's Commission, *A New Era*, 23.

34. Dillon, "Labeled."

35. April 6, 1994. See the Office for Civil Rights focus on the overidentification of minority students.

36. 20 USC 1401 (c)(12)(A)–(E). Also see *New York Times*, "Special Education and Minorities," November 20, 2005.

37. Thomas A. Mayes and Perry A. Zirkel, "Special Education Tuition Reimbursement Claims: An Empirical Analysis," *Remedial and Special Education* 22, no. 6 (2001): 350.

38. *Doe v. Board of Education of the Tullahoma City Schools*, 20 IDELR 617 (6th Cir. 1993).

39. 546 U.S. 49 (2005).

40. Christopher Borreca, "The Adversarial Process: Does It Help or Hurt Our Mission?" *Leadership Insider*, November 2006 (National School Board Association); citing D. Neal and D. Kirp, "The Allure of Legalization Reconsidered: The Case of Special Education," in D. Kirp and D. Jensen, eds., *School Days, Rule Days: The Legalization and Regulation of Education* (New York: Falmer Press, 1986). See also Stephen M. R. Covey, *The Speed of Trust: The One Thing That Changes Everything* (New York: Free Press, 2006).

41. Common Good, www.commongood.org.

42. Mohl and Sullivan, "Isn't Every Child Special?"

43. Tyce Palmaffy, "The Evolution of the Federal Role," in Finn et al., *Rethinking Special Education*, 19.

44. Brookings Institution, www.brookings.edu; American Institute of Research, www.air.org. Other studies mentioned in this list have been cited in earlier notes.

45. This is not a proposal to end other litigation. It focuses only on disputes about programming—i.e., FAPE.

46. In "The Evolution of the Federal Role," Tyce Palmaffy asks why SLD students *"are more deserving of extra*

help than everyday low achievers" (p. 8). Mark Kelman, in "The Moral Foundations of Special Education Law," in Finn et al., *Rethinking Special Education*, states: "*In a world of limited resources, it is plainly not enough to say that children with learning disabilities 'deserve' more resources; their claims inevitably compete with claims that could be made by other 'deserving' pupils who can be described in a wide variety of ways (such as poor achievers, socioeconomically disadvantaged, and gifted but understimulated)*" (p. 82). Also, in "Conclusions and Principles for Reform" (in Finn et al., *Rethinking Special Education*), Chester E. Finn Jr., Andrew J. Rotherham, and Charles R. Hokanson Jr. recommend a "full airing" of why SLD students have a greater entitlement to education resources than other students (p. 344).

47. "Extra-Special Education at Public Expense," *San Francisco Chronicle*, February 19, 2006, 1.

48. Daniel McGroarty, "The Little-Known Case of America's Largest School Choice Program," in Finn et al., *Rethinking Special Education*, 289–307.

49. For example, in Massachusetts, of the more than 600 requests for hearings per year, most of which deal with disputes about FAPE, only 30 to 40 disputes go to a hearing and receive a hearing officer decision. That is a mere 5% to 7% of all hearing requests. Many of the rest settle, often by cost-share agreements. Since no data are available about why and how cases settle, this assertion is based on anecdotal evidence.

50. Zirkel, "Over-Legalization of Special Education," March 24, 2005, 36, citing "The 'Explosion' in Education Litigation: An Update," 114 Ed. Law Rep. (1997): 9341–9351.

51. Kevin J. Lanigan, Rose Marie L. Audette, Alexander E. Dreier, and Maya R. Kobersy, "Nasty, Brutish . . . and Often Not Very Short: The Attorney Perspective on Due Process," in Finn et al., *Rethinking Special Education*, 213–231.

52. 557 U.S. ____ (2009).

53. Kim Goodrich Ratcliffe, Ed.D., testimony at "IDEA: What's Good for Kids? What Works for Schools?" Senate Health, Education, Labor and Pensions Committee hearing, March 21, 2002, http://ftp.resource.org/gpo.gov/hearings/107s/78448.pdf.

54. For a model of such a solution, see SpedEx, the innovative pilot program in Massachusetts (www.doe.mass.edu/bsea/spedx.html).

55. Howard, *Life without Lawyers*, 64.

56. Ibid., 65.

57. Ibid., introduction, 11.

58. Palmaffy, "Evolution of the Federal Role," 15.

59. Thomas Hehir and Sue Gamm, "Special Education: From Legalism to Collaboration," in *Law and School Reform* (New Haven, CT: Yale University Press, 1999), 215, cited in Finn et al., *Rethinking Special Education*, 15–16.

60. Sheri Klein, "Reducing Special Education Paperwork," in *Principal*, September–October 2004, www.naesp.org. See also Westat's Study of Personnel Needs in Special Education, http://ferdig.coe.ufl.edu/spense. Notably, this report was cited by the Supreme Court in *Schaffer v. Weast*. The paperwork burden is a huge problem.

61. Special Education Day, www.specialeducationday.com.

62. Borreca, "Adversarial Process."

63. National Council on Disability, *Back to School on Civil Rights* (2000), www.ncd.gov/newsroom/publications/2000/pdf/backtoschool.pdf.

64. Ratcliffe testimony.

65. More information about Procedures Lite is found at www.specialeducationday.com.

66. Chester E. Finn Jr., Andrew J. Rotherham, and Charles R. Hokanson Jr., "Conclusions and Principles for Reform," in Finn et al., *Rethinking Special Education*, 336.

67. Among many books on the subject, see Christina Hoff Sommers and Sally Satel, M.D., *One Nation under Therapy* (New York: St. Martin's Press, 2005), 53, which contains this passage: *"The therapeutic regime pathologizes healthy young people. It encourages remedial measures for nonexisting vulnerabilities, wastes students' time, and impedes their academic and moral development. American students are, with few exceptions, mentally and emotionally sound; they are resilient. They need more, not less, homework. They can cope with dodgeball."* The mention of dodgeball refers to the fact that many schools no longer allow that playground game during recess, believing that it is dangerous and threatens children's self-esteem. Unfortunately, many schools don't allow recess at all. For example, see the November 20, 2004, MSNBC story of a lawsuit in New York about dodgeball's safety on school playgrounds, www.msnbc.msn.com/id/6535954.

68. Carol Dweck, *Mindset: The New Psychology of Success* (New York: Ballantine Books, 2006).

69. See also Matthew B. Crawford, "The Case for Working with Your Hands," *New York Times*, May 24, 2009, www.nytimes.com/2009/05/24/magazine/24labor-t.html.

70. Daniel Coyle, *The Talent Code: Greatness Isn't Born. It's Grown. Here's How* (New York: Bantam Books, 2009).

71. Institute for the Future of the Mind, www.futuremind.ox.ac.uk.

72. Byrnes, *Taking Sides*, xxvii.

73. Lyon et al., "Rethinking Learning Disabilities," 259, 268–269, 282.

74. See, e.g., Dwyer, "Rights without Labels,'" 36. Dwyer argues for a critical change *"away from labels and to effective intervention services for all children."*

75. Thus, schools promote "best practices" among all teachers; schools are to use universal design principles, by

which school buildings, classroom materials, textbooks, etc., are designed to be accessible to as many types of learners as possible (without lowering standards). See, e.g., www.ed.gov/about/offices/list/ovae/pi/AdultEd/disaccess.html.

76. Robert J. Sternberg and Elena L. Grigorenko, *Our Labeled Children* (Cambridge, MA: Perseus, 1999), 257.

77. "Introduction to a New Era," in President's Commission, *A New Era*, 23.

78. Asbridge, "Does It Work?"

79. UNESCO, *"Inclusive Education: The Way of the Future": Conclusions and Recommendations of the 48th Session of the International Conference on Education (ICE)* (2008), www.ibe.unesco.org/en/ice/48th-ice-2008.html.

80. Lisa Belkin, "Let the Kid Be," *New York Times*, May 31, 2009.

81. Palmaffy, "Evolution of the Federal Role," 15; the National Council on Disability report cited by Palmaffy is *Back to School on Civil Rights*.

82. McGroarty, "Little-Known Case," 293–294.

83. For an interesting analysis of the effects of incentives in public policy, see Steven D. Levitt and Stephen J. Dubner, *Freakonomics: A Rogue Economist Explores the Hidden Side of Everything* (New York: William Morrow, 2005).

84. Barack Obama, campaign speech, May 27, 2008, www.denverpost.com/news/ci_9405199.

85. See, e.g., www.plainlanguage.gov and www.plainlanguage.org.

86. Bill Cosby and Alvin F. Poussaint, M.D., *Come On, People: On the Path from Victims to Victors* (Nashville, TN: Thomas Nelson, 2007).

87. Paul Tough, "What It Takes to Make a Student," *New York Times Magazine*, November 26, 2006.

88. UNESCO, *"Inclusive Education,"* 3–4.

89. A whole book can be written about the use of one-on-one aides in our nation's classrooms to monitor SWD included in general education classrooms and to make the system "work." Questions about this controversial and costly approach and its efficacy in promoting the only goal that matters—improved learning—are widespread. But we leave that book for another day.

90. The Principals' Partnership, "Inclusion/Least Restrictive Environment," www.principalspartnership.com/inclusionlre.pdf.

91. Similar concerns have been raised in the United Kingdom. See, e.g., "School Inclusion Policies Not Working, Says Report," *Guardian*, October 12, 2004.

92. 347 U.S. 483 (1954).

93. Lowell C. Rose and Alec M. Gallup, "The 36th Annual Phi DeltaKappa/Gallup Poll of the Public's Attitudes toward the Public Schools," *Phi Delta Kappan* 86, no. 1 (2004), www.pdkmembers.org/members_online/publications/e-GALLUP/kpoll_pdfs/pdkpoll36_2004.pdf.

94. See, e.g., Mayes and Zirkel, *Special Education Tuition Reimbursement Claims*; and Robert Tomsho, "Parents of Disabled Students Push for Separate Classes," *Wall Street Journal*, November 27, 2007. See also Amy Dockser Marcus, "Eli's Choice," *Wall Street Journal*, December 31, 2005.

95. James M. Kauffman and Daniel P. Hallahan, *The Illusion of Full Inclusion: A Comprehensive Critique of a Current Special Education Bandwagon*, 2nd ed. (Austin, TX: Pro-Ed, 2005).

96. James W. Stigler and James Hiebert, *The Teaching Gap* (New York: Free Press, 1999).

97. Sternberg and Grigorenko, *Our Labeled Children*, 88.

98. See, e.g., a popular book that celebrates strengths for four- to eight-year-olds that many teachers use in their classrooms: *Stand Tall, Molly Lou Melon*, by Patty Lovell (New York: Putnam, 2001).

99. For more information about Buckingham, visit www.marcusbuckingham.com.

100. Paul Orfalea, "Introduction: How to Succeed in Business without Really Reading," in *Copy This! Lessons from a Hyperactive Dyslexic Who Turned a Bright Idea into One of America's Best Companies* (New York: Workman, 2005), xix.

101. Alison L. Fraser, *Vocational-Technical Education in Massachusetts* (Boston: Pioneer Institute, 2008), www.pioneerinstitute.org/pdf/wp42.pdf.

102. Joe Lamacchia and Bridget Samburg, *Blue Collar and Proud of It: The All-in-One Resource for Finding Freedom, Financial Success, and Security outside the Cubicle* (Deerfield Beach, FL: Health Communications, 2009), www.bluecollarandproudofit.com.

103. See also the All Kinds of Minds institute, www.allkindsofminds.org; and Mel Levine, M.D., *A Mind at a Time: America's Top Learning Expert Shows How Every Child Can Succeed* (New York: Simon and Schuster, 2002).

104. Albert Shanker, "Congress Remakes a Law," *New York Times*, July 10, 1994, http://source.nysut.org/weblink7/DocView.aspx?id=1009.

105. Coyle, *Talent Code*, 44.

106. Jonah Lehrer, "The Truth about Grit," *Boston Globe*, August 2, 2009, www.boston.com/bostonglobe/ideas/articles/2009/08/02/the_truth_about_grit/.

107. See the Resiliency Center, with its tagline "The Power to Bounce Back," at www.resiliencycenter.com; and the Global Resiliency Network at www.globalresiliency.net.

108. Harold W. Stevenson and James W. Stigler, *The Learning Gap* (New York: Simon and Schuster, 1992), preface.

109. UNESCO, *"Inclusive Education,"* 4.

110. Cited in Byrnes, *Taking Sides*, Issue 12.

111. For more information, see Miriam Kurtzig Freedman, *Student Testing and the Law* and *Grades, Report Cards, Etc. . . . and the Law*, www.schoollawpro.com and www.parkplacepubs.com.

112. Sternberg and Grigorenko, *Our Labeled Children*, 88–89.

113. Law professor Mark Kelman reviews some of the issues related to accommodations: *"Whatever one's view of testing accommodation, determinations of what skills are appropriate to test and what can and cannot be justly tested and rewarded are policy issues. Casting them as issues of discrimination—do those with disabilities have the opportunity to succeed on tests?—assumes naively that norms against discrimination mandate equality of group outcome, rather than that inequalities be justified by real distinctions in relevant performance."* Kelman, "Moral Foundations of Special Education Law," 80–81.

114. 20 USC 1401.

115. www.ldadvocates.com/RedFlagReadingScreen.html.

116. See John Hechinger and Daniel Golden, "When Special Education Goes Too Easy on Students: Parents Say Schools Game System, Let Kids Graduate without Skills," *Wall Street Journal*, August 21, 2007.

117. Sternberg and Grigorenko, *Our Labeled Children*, 89.

118. Secretary Arne Duncan, speaking at the National Press Club, May 29, 2009, www.press.org.

119. *Montgomery Township Board of Education*, 43 IDELR 186 (3rd Cir. 2005), unpublished decision.

120. Diane Ravitch, "Time to Kill 'No Child Left Behind,'" *Education Week*, June 10, 2009, www.edweek.org.

121. www.edweek.org/ew/articles/1996/01/31/19letter.h15.html.

122. Mohl and Sullivan, "Isn't Every Child Special?"

123. Ibid.

124. John Cloud, "Are We Failing Our Geniuses?" *Time* cover story August 16, 2007, www.time.com/time/printout/0,8816,1653653,00.html.

125. Palmaffy, "Evolution of the Federal Role," 8.

126. See *Time*, January 24, 2005, cover story, "Meet the Twixters": "Meet the twixters, young adults who live off their parents, bounce from job to job and hop from mate to mate. They're not lazy . . . THEY JUST WON'T GROW UP."

127. Scott E. Carrell and Mark L. Hoekstra, "Domino Effect," *Education Next*, Summer 2009, http://educationnext.org/domino-effect-2/.

128. Kelman, "Moral Foundations of Special Education Law," 78. See also Howard, *Life without Lawyers*; and Sternberg and Grigorenko, *Our Labeled Children*.

129. Miriam Kurtzig Freedman, "The Elevator Theory of Special Education," *Education Week*, February 15, 1995.

130. Kelman, "Moral Foundations of Special Education Law," 82, 84.

131. Miriam Kurtzig Freedman, "Disabling the SAT: The College Board Undermines Its Premier Test," *Education Next*, Fall

2003, www.schoollawpro.com or http://educationnext.org/disablingthesat/. See also ABC News, "SAT Help," March 31, 2006, video report, http://abcnews.go.com/video/playerIndex?id=1789267.

132. Kelman, "Moral Foundations of Special Education Law," 78–80.

133. McKinsey and Co., *The Economic Impact of the Achievement Gap in America's Schools* (2009), www.mckinsey.com/clientservices/socialsector.

134. Sheldon Berman, Perry Davis, Ann Koufman-Frederick, and David Urion, "The Rising Costs of Special Education in Massachusetts: Causes and Effects," in Finn et al., *Rethinking Special Education*. But see Marcus A. Winters and Jay P. Greene, "Debunking a Special Education Myth," *Education Next*, Spring 2007, http://educationnext.org/debunking-a-special-education-myth/. Note that this study focuses on private school placement costs. Clearly, cost issues are complicated, a complication that, in itself, may be miring us down.

135. President's Commission, *A New Era.*

136. Mohl and Sullivan, "Isn't Every Child Special?"

137. Jan Davidson and Bob Davidson, with Laura Vanderkam, *Genius Denied: How to Stop Wasting Our Brightest Young Minds* (New York: Simon and Schuster, 2004), 16.

138. "Remarks of President Barack Obama—As Prepared for Delivery Address to Joint Session of Congress Tuesday, February 24th, 2009," www.whitehouse.gov/the_press_office/remarks-of-president-barack-obama-address-to-joint-session-of-congress/.

139. Cosby and Poussaint, *Come On, People.*

140. See, e.g., Special Education Day, www.specialeducationday.com.

Acknowledgments

Thank you! You—my colleagues, clients, friends, and thought leaders. Not all of you share my views about special education, as this is a controversial arena, but I believe we all share the commitment to improve education for all children. Sharing our experiences and the passion for doing the right thing for students led me to write this book. We work in a challenging arena—improving public education and protecting individual student rights. I am grateful for the many participants at my seminars, keynotes, and consultations who provided me with wonderful stories, insight, and hope—as together we work for better schools for all students. It is time for us to transform the special education system we now have. Together, we must!

The views and opinions in this *little flipbook* are mine. I thank my colleagues and friends at Stoneman, Chandler & Miller LLP for their continued support. I am grateful for the insights, challenges, encouragement, and friendship of so many others who helped me make this book real—in particular, Marilyn Bisbicos, Sari Brown, Elizabeth Chadis, David Driscoll, Jamie Gass, Rick Hanushek, Philip K. Howard, Carla B. Jentz, Marcia Kastner, Mark LeBlanc, Candace McCann, Edward Orenstein, Jerome Schultz, Jim Shillinglaw, Jim Walsh, and the Texas team: editor Rosemary Wetherold, book designer David Timmons, and copublisher Ted Siff of Park Place Publications. Of course, there's a risk in writing this list, as I may be leaving out others who should be included. The reality is that I am so grateful for all friends and colleagues—both named and unnamed—who helped get this book out there. And, of course, I am most grateful for Dan, Julie, and Paul.

Readers' comments are welcome. Please e-mail me at miriam@schoollawpro.com.

About the Author

Attorney Miriam Kurtzig Freedman works with people who want better schools, helps practitioners move from confusion to confidence when dealing with legal requirements, and promotes school reform. As an immigrant to America at elementary-school age, she was empowered by America's public schools. Now she helps educators get back to the mission of teaching *all* children.

Miriam, a school attorney, is of counsel to the Boston law firm of Stoneman, Chandler & Miller LLP. She provides clients and national audiences with lively and practical keynotes, training, and consultation. Information about her books, articles, and blog is available on her website at www.schoollawpro.com. A former teacher, Miriam "gets it"—what school folks, parents, and other stakeholders need to know and do to help all students learn. She cofounded Special Education Day, celebrated annually on December 2 (www.specialeducationday.com), and the Special Education Day Committee (SPEDCO) to spur special education reform.

Miriam received her law degree from New York University, her masters from the State University of New York, Stony Brook, and her bachelor of arts from Barnard College (Columbia University). During the winter term, she is a visiting fellow at Stanford University.

School Law Pro develops and publishes the *little flipbooks* series and other products. Its books provide practical, informative, and fun legal and policy information—in plain English. The focus of the *little flipbooks* is to assist educators, parents, policymakers, and others in furthering the mission of improving teaching and learning for all students in our schools.

School Law Pro
www.schoollawpro.com

Park Place Publications publishes books, DVDs, and additional resources for educators and others interested in education. We are dedicated to helping the people who help students and to contributing to the creation of a first-class education system for all students.

Park Place Publications
www.parkplacepubs.com

School Law Pro and Park Place Publications welcome your comments, questions, and concerns. Readers interested in Ms. Freedman's presentations, keynotes, and consultation may contact her at miriam@schoollawpro.com. Park Place Publications may be reached at info@parkplacepubs.com.